How to get into

The best g ectures!

Ah, university. It's a e the deadline
and having deep until 3 a.m.

In short, there's a wh so you'll want
to sleep with this in the post.

It's packed with e journey,
from picking the p chever unis
you're applyi alents!

By the way, this code only works for one person. If somebody else has used
this book before you, they might have already claimed the Online Edition.

Contents

Published by CGP

Editors:
Siân Butler, Andy Cashmore, Rebecca Greaves, Sean Walsh

With thanks to Tom Carney and Robert Rastelli for the proofreading.
With thanks to Emily Smith for the copyright research.

Data used on page 2 from the Graduate Labour Market Statistics 2018 report contains public se[...]
the Open Government Licence v3.0. http://www.nationalarchives.gov.uk/doc/open-governmen[...]

Please note that this book is not endorsed by the Universities and Colleges Admissions Service (U[...]ay.

ISBN: 978 1 78908 555 6   Printed by Elanders Ltd, Newcastle upon Tyne.

Clipart from Corel®
Based on the classic CGP style created by Richard Parsons.

How To Use This Book

There's a lot to consider when applying to university. Use this page to get an idea of everything you'll need to do and consider, and then dive into each section of the book to get all the juicy details. University ahoy!

Here's a Map to Guide You Through The Book

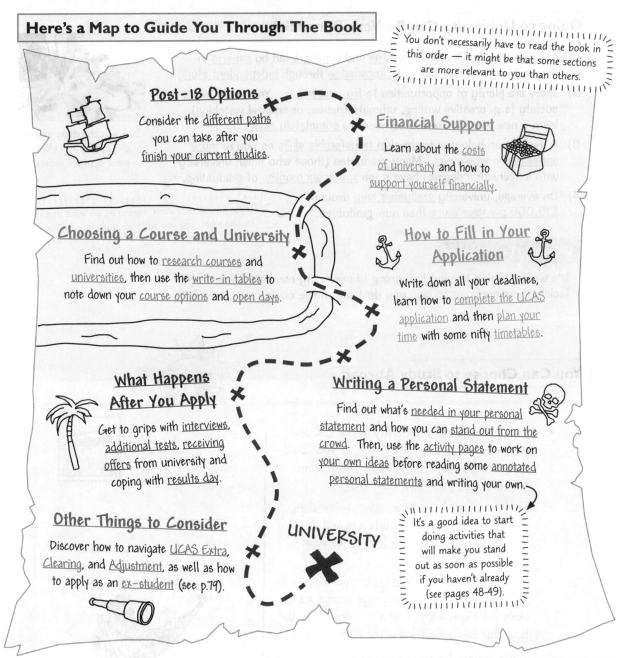

You don't necessarily have to read the book in this order — it might be that some sections are more relevant to you than others.

Post-18 Options

Consider the different paths you can take after you finish your current studies.

Financial Support

Learn about the costs of university and how to support yourself financially.

Choosing a Course and University

Find out how to research courses and universities, then use the write-in tables to note down your course options and open days.

How to Fill in Your Application

Write down all your deadlines, learn how to complete the UCAS application and then plan your time with some nifty timetables.

What Happens After You Apply

Get to grips with interviews, additional tests, receiving offers from university and coping with results day.

Writing a Personal Statement

Find out what's needed in your personal statement and how you can stand out from the crowd. Then, use the activity pages to work on your own ideas before reading some annotated personal statements and writing your own.

Other Things to Consider

Discover how to navigate UCAS Extra, Clearing, and Adjustment, as well as how to apply as an ex-student (see p.79).

UNIVERSITY

It's a good idea to start doing activities that will make you stand out as soon as possible if you haven't already (see pages 48-49).

The next thing to do with this book is to turn the page in about 10 seconds...

Try not to feel too overwhelmed by how much you have to do. This book has split everything into manageable chunks so that you can take it one step at a time and eventually reach the treasure that is getting into university.

University

Don't worry if you're not completely sure what you want to do after college — this section covers a range of options that are available to you. Up first we have 'going to university', which is surprising for this book...

Going to University Can Be Very Beneficial

1) At university, you'll attend <u>lectures</u> and <u>seminars</u> led by <u>experts</u> in your subject and <u>increase your knowledge</u> through <u>independent study</u>.

2) There are plenty of opportunities to <u>try new things</u>. You could join a society (e.g. creative writing, ultimate frisbee, or squirrel watching), learn a new language or live somewhere <u>completely new</u>.

3) A degree can help you to <u>develop transferable skills</u> so you're <u>more appealing</u> to <u>employers</u>. Many graduates (those who finish university with a bachelor's degree) have a job <u>within six months</u> of graduating.

4) On average, university <u>graduates earn</u> around <u>£10,000 per year more</u> than non-graduates.

Sam was regretting joining the 'staring at a blank piece of paper' society.

These figures may differ depending on what degree you do and what jobs you want to apply for after university.

University Costs Money

It's worth bearing in mind that going to university can be <u>expensive</u>, but luckily there are <u>ways to help</u> you deal with these costs (see <u>pages 8-11</u>).

You Can Choose to Study Abroad

- You might choose a university in the UK and go abroad as <u>part of your course</u>, or you could choose to do your <u>whole degree</u> at a foreign university (see <u>page 25</u>).

- Studying abroad can be a <u>culturally-enriching experience</u>. It can allow you to see and do things that are <u>completely different</u> to what you're used to.

- It's a chance to <u>learn or improve</u> your <u>language skills</u>. If you're doing a language course, it's likely you'll spend <u>a year</u> in a country where the language you're studying is the native language.

- You also have the chance to <u>make friends</u> from different cultures and countries.

AIRMAIL

University

Think About Why You Want to Go to University

1) It can be <u>easy to drift</u> towards applying to university without really thinking about it, but while a degree from a university can open up <u>more opportunities</u> to you, it's <u>not a guaranteed path</u> to success.

2) Other options (like apprenticeships, internships, NVQs and entry-level jobs) might provide you with a <u>better route</u> to achieving your <u>goals</u> — there's more about these on pages 4-5.

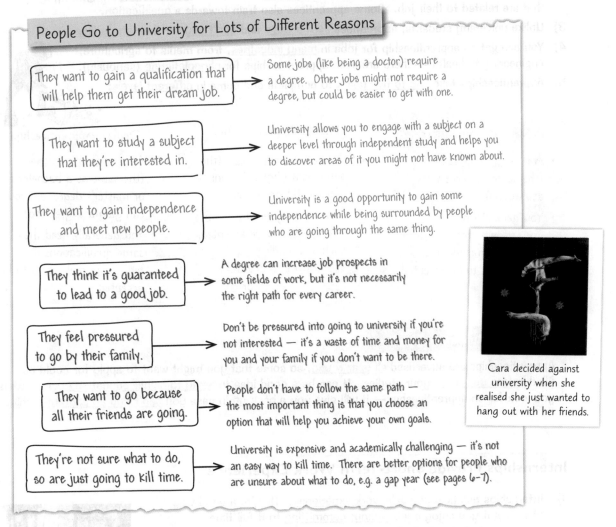

People Go to University for Lots of Different Reasons

They want to gain a qualification that will help them get their dream job. → Some jobs (like being a doctor) require a degree. Other jobs might not require a degree, but could be easier to get with one.

They want to study a subject that they're interested in. → University allows you to engage with a subject on a deeper level through independent study and helps you to discover areas of it you might not have known about.

They want to gain independence and meet new people. → University is a good opportunity to gain some independence while being surrounded by people who are going through the same thing.

They think it's guaranteed to lead to a good job. → A degree can increase job prospects in some fields of work, but it's not necessarily the right path for every career.

They feel pressured to go by their family. → Don't be pressured into going to university if you're not interested — it's a waste of time and money for you and your family if you don't want to be there.

They want to go because all their friends are going. → People don't have to follow the same path — the most important thing is that you choose an option that will help you achieve your own goals.

They're not sure what to do, so are just going to kill time. → University is expensive and academically challenging — it's not an easy way to kill time. There are better options for people who are unsure about what to do, e.g. a gap year (see pages 6-7).

Cara decided against university when she realised she just wanted to hang out with her friends.

3) The <u>best reason</u> to go to university is because <u>you</u> want to go — think about <u>what you want</u> to do in the future and <u>whether university can help you to achieve it</u>.

University is about hitting the books — just try not to hurt your hand...

Allow me to be serious for a moment. My degree helped me to get this job writing silly jokes and drawing funny pictures. It just proves that university can lead you to great success if you want to become a master of hilarity...

Apprenticeships and Internships

Yes, this book is about applying to university, and there is lots of information about how to do that coming up, but there are other options you can consider too. Let's set sail with the apprentice and intern ships...

Apprenticeships Let You Train While You Work

1) Apprenticeships are great if you <u>know what career</u> you want and you're <u>eager</u> to <u>start working</u>.

2) Apprentices get <u>on-the-job experience</u> in a <u>workplace</u> as well as <u>time to study</u> things that are related to their job. Some apprentices also train towards a <u>qualification</u>.

3) Unlike university students, apprentices <u>earn a wage</u> and <u>don't pay</u> for their <u>study time</u>.

4) You can get an apprenticeship for jobs in <u>many industries</u>, from media to agriculture, engineering to health — there are even apprenticeships for <u>chocolatiering</u> (seriously).

5) Apprenticeships take <u>one to five years</u> to complete and come in <u>different levels</u>:

Advanced Apprenticeship

- A <u>Level 3 qualification</u> (the same as two passes at A-Level).
- You generally need <u>five GCSEs</u> with <u>grades 9 to 4</u> (A* to C), including <u>English and Maths</u>, to be accepted.

Higher Apprenticeship

- A <u>Level 4 qualification</u> (the same as a Higher National Certificate) or above.
- You generally need a <u>Level 3 qualification</u> to be accepted, such as an <u>advanced apprenticeship</u> or certain <u>A-Levels</u>, <u>NVQs</u> or <u>BTECs</u>.

Degree Apprenticeship

- A <u>Level 6 or 7 qualification</u> (the same as a bachelor's or master's degree — you can gain a degree too).
- You generally need the same qualifications as a <u>higher apprenticeship</u> to be accepted.

Deadlines for Apprenticeships Vary

Apprenticeships are advertised <u>all year round</u>, so some that you might want to apply for could be filled <u>before you finish</u> your studies. It can be a good idea to <u>apply to higher education courses</u> while you look for an apprenticeship — it will give you a <u>back up</u> in case you <u>can't find an apprenticeship</u>.

Internships Provide Short-Term Work Experience

1) Internships can help you <u>gain work experience</u>. They're a good way of seeing if you enjoy a job <u>without committing</u> to it full time.

2) Internships are <u>relatively short</u> (they usually last between a week and a few months). They're <u>sometimes unpaid</u>, and usually even paid internships <u>don't pay much</u> — they're not really used long term.

3) The level of <u>responsibility</u> you have in an internship can <u>vary</u>. Some internships will <u>give you work</u> to do, while others will have you <u>shadow a professional</u> to observe how they do their job.

Carlos knew his new boss would be impressed with his shadowing skills.

NVQs and Entry-Level Jobs

National Vocational Qualifications (NVQs) and entry-level jobs are good options if you know what job you're after and you prefer work-based learning. Sadly, there aren't any for 'panda hugging expert' — sigh...

NVQs Are Specific Job Qualifications

NVQs are courses that are tailored to <u>particular jobs</u>. They test skills through <u>work-related tasks</u> and are run in a <u>college</u>, <u>school</u> or <u>workplace</u>. Here's some more information about them:

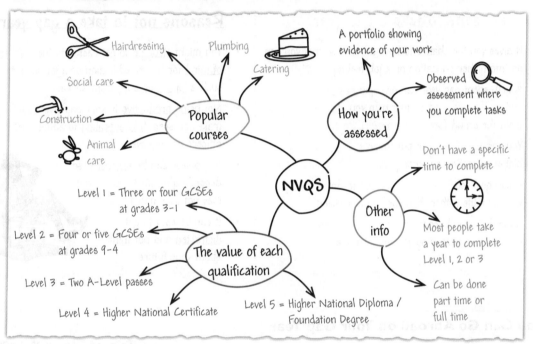

Hairdressing   Plumbing
Catering
Social care
Construction
Animal care

Popular courses

A portfolio showing evidence of your work

How you're assessed

Observed assessment where you complete tasks

NVQS

Don't have a specific time to complete

Other info

Most people take a year to complete Level 1, 2 or 3

Can be done part time or full time

Level 1 = Three or four GCSEs at grades 3-1

Level 2 = Four or five GCSEs at grades 9-4

The value of each qualification

Level 3 = Two A-Level passes

Level 4 = Higher National Certificate

Level 5 = Higher National Diploma / Foundation Degree

Going Straight Into Work is an Option

1) If you <u>don't want to study</u> anymore, or you're <u>keen to start work</u>, an <u>entry-level job</u> might be a good option. You <u>don't need</u> any <u>previous experience</u> and you <u>train on the job</u> while <u>earning a wage</u>.

2) However, some jobs <u>require</u> higher-level qualifications. Before discounting further study, see what <u>qualifications</u> you <u>need</u> for your <u>dream job</u>.

3) To keep <u>building your skills</u>, look out for vacancies that offer the following:

   • <u>Training</u> related to your career sector or towards <u>qualifications</u>

   • **Opportunities** for <u>promotions</u> and <u>career progression</u>

   • A variety of <u>different</u> day-to-day <u>tasks</u>

John wasn't sure about the training he received in his new fashion job.

And you thought deciding what to have for tea tonight was tricky...

There are a lot of post-18 options out there, and they might leave you feeling overwhelmed. Speaking to one of your tutors or a careers advisor at school or college may help you to decide what's best for you to do next.

Taking a Gap Year

If you're unsure about what to do after your studies, a gap year can give you time to reflect. Just don't spend it lazing around, otherwise you'll fall into a chasm of idleness — that's the worst kind of gap year...

Think About Whether a Gap Year is Right For You

A gap year can benefit you in many ways, but you need to be wary of potential pitfalls:

Reasons to take a gap year

- It gives you the chance to have a break so that you can go into higher education or a job feeling revitalised.
- A well-spent gap year can give you new skills and unique experiences that help you stand out from the crowd (see pages 48-49).
- You can earn money to put towards higher education or other plans.
- It can give you time to decide what to do with your life rather than rushing a decision.
- It can help you become more confident and independent, preparing you for later life.

Reasons not to take a gap year

- You might struggle to get back into the right frame of mind for higher education or a job after taking such a long time away from working.
- Not being productive in your gap year could make you seem less appealing to admissions officers or employers.
- A gap year can be expensive, so depending on what you do, you may not save much money.

- It can be easy to get distracted and not think about your future.

You Can Go Abroad on Your Gap Year

1) Travelling around foreign countries can be rewarding:
   - It can let you see and experience different cultures.
   - It can show future employers that you have transferable skills — arranging your own travel and accommodation will help demonstrate your planning and budgeting skills.
   - It can improve your language skills.
2) You can get a job abroad, such as teaching English as a foreign language. These jobs can help fund your travels.
3) You can also volunteer abroad. There are companies that organise volunteering trips, but check whether the work you'd be doing will definitely help the local community.

Things to consider if you want to go abroad

- How much you need to pay for flights, accommodation, food, visas and insurance.
- How long you want to be away from home for.
- How safe your destination is.
- How reliable any company or volunteer group is.

For example, sometimes having unskilled volunteers on construction projects takes jobs away from locals, and it can leave villages with unsustainable infrastructure, which can cause long-term problems.

Taking a Gap Year

There Are Also Many Opportunities in the UK

Although gap years are often associated with going abroad, there are lots of <u>opportunities closer to home</u> as well. These <u>different opportunities</u> can <u>benefit you</u> in a variety of ways:

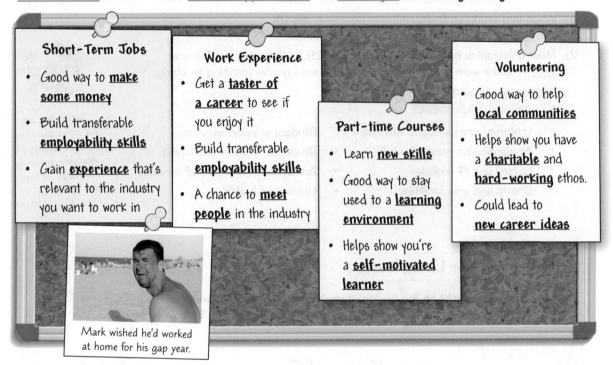

Short-Term Jobs

- Good way to **make some money**
- Build transferable **employability skills**
- Gain **experience** that's relevant to the industry you want to work in

Work Experience

- Get a **taster of a career** to see if you enjoy it
- Build transferable **employability skills**
- A chance to **meet people** in the industry

Part-time Courses

- Learn **new skills**
- Good way to stay used to a **learning environment**
- Helps show you're a **self-motivated learner**

Volunteering

- Good way to help **local communities**
- Helps show you have a **charitable** and **hard-working** ethos.
- Could lead to **new career ideas**

Mark wished he'd worked at home for his gap year.

You Can Defer Entry to University If You're Taking a Gap Year

1) If you definitely want to go to university, but you also want to take a gap year, you can apply for <u>deferred entry</u> through UCAS. This means you'll start your course <u>a year later</u> than normal.

> If you're applying to a conservatoire (see page 27), you'll need to contact them directly about deferred entry rather than through your UCAS application.

2) You'll have to <u>explain</u> in your <u>personal statement</u> why you're deferring a year — if you <u>don't</u> have a <u>good reason</u>, then universities might be <u>less likely</u> to <u>accept you</u>.

3) To be accepted, you'll still have to <u>meet the entry requirements</u> for your <u>offer</u> in the <u>year you apply</u>.

4) You <u>won't be able</u> to defer entry on <u>some courses</u> — if you plan to defer, you should <u>check</u> that the university is <u>happy</u> to let you defer <u>before submitting</u> your application.

5) You can also <u>wait to apply</u> to university until <u>during or after</u> your gap year (see <u>page 79</u>).

I bought and sold novelty clocks during my gap year — it was time well spent...

To make sure your gap year has a purpose, write down three things you'll do or three skills you'll gain that will impress a university or employer. That way, you won't be stuck when it comes to writing your personal statement.

The Costs of Going to University

Thinking about the costs of university can sometimes feel like climbing a mountain with a heavy backpack in the middle of a storm. Try not to worry though — after these pages you'll feel like a mountain goat.

You'll Need to Pay University Tuition Fees...

1) When you study an <u>undergraduate degree</u> in the UK, you <u>pay tuition fees</u> for each year of your course.

2) Most universities in the UK charge around £9,250 a year, but this can <u>vary</u> — make sure you <u>check the fees</u> at places you're planning to study.

What Tuition Fees Pay for

- Lectures, seminars and tutorials
- Academic and research staff
- Library and IT facilities
- Sports and arts facilities
- Student support services
- Students' Union membership
- Administration staff and services
- Upkeep of buildings

Tuition fees are expensive, but there is financial support available, including a tuition fee loan (see p.10).

...As Well As Your Living Costs

Going to university might be the <u>first time</u> you've had to deal with some of the <u>main costs of living</u>. Here are some of the <u>basic expenses</u> you'll need to be able to cover:

1 <u>Accommodation and bills</u>

- You'll need to <u>pay rent</u> for <u>student accommodation</u> or a <u>private property</u>. You might have to <u>pay bills</u> as well.
- <u>Living at home</u> can be a <u>cheaper</u> option.

2 <u>Food and drink</u>

- <u>Catered accommodation</u> provides most meals, but <u>can be more expensive</u> than self-catered accommodation.
- If you go <u>self-catered</u>, you'll need to <u>budget more</u> to spend on food.

3 <u>Toiletries and clothing</u>

- It's easy to forget about these, but they're <u>necessary</u>.
- You can <u>keep costs down</u> by buying toiletries in discount shops and only buying clothes when you need them.

The cost of living is one of the things you should consider when choosing a university (see p.23).

Sarah's dad wasn't convinced by her latest 'essential' purchase.

Living costs can be covered in a variety of ways, including a maintenance loan and other types of financial support (see p.10-11).

The Costs of Going to University

Basic living expenses might seem obvious, but you probably want to have some money so you can do other things too. Here are some other expenses you'll encounter at uni, and some useful tips to keep costs down.

Here Are Some Extra Costs

Extra Course Costs

- <u>Textbooks</u> / <u>stationery</u>
- A <u>laptop</u>
- <u>Printing</u>
- <u>Specialist equipment</u>
- <u>Field trips</u>

Transport

- <u>Public transport</u>
- <u>Commuting</u> to and from university
- <u>Travelling home and back</u> between terms

Free Time

- <u>Sports</u> and <u>societies</u>
- <u>Eating out</u>
- <u>Shopping</u>
- <u>Entertainment services</u>, e.g. TV subscriptions

There Are Ways to Keep Costs Down

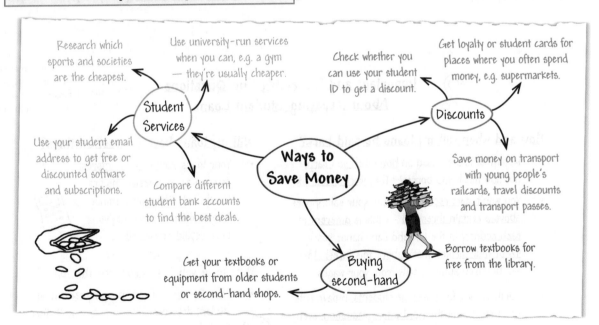

Research which sports and societies are the cheapest.

Use university-run services when you can, e.g. a gym — they're usually cheaper.

Check whether you can use your student ID to get a discount.

Get loyalty or student cards for places where you often spend money, e.g. supermarkets.

Use your student email address to get free or discounted software and subscriptions.

Student Services

Compare different student bank accounts to find the best deals.

Ways to Save Money

Discounts

Save money on transport with young people's railcards, travel discounts and transport passes.

Buying second-hand

Borrow textbooks for free from the library.

Get your textbooks or equipment from older students or second-hand shops.

My friend nailed his wallet to the floor — it helped him keep costs down...

There are high costs associated with going to university, but there are plenty of ways to save money that you can take advantage of. The less you have to worry about money, the more you'll be able to enjoy studying.

Financial Support

Most students who go to university take out loans with Student Finance to help support them through their studies. It might seem daunting, but this handy page breaks it down into bite-size pieces for you. Yum...

There Are Two Types of Loan Available

Student Finance offers a tuition fee loan (to cover the full cost of tuition) and a maintenance loan (to help pay for living costs). Most students are eligible for both loans.

Tuition fee loans

- You're likely to be eligible for this if you're a UK student on an approved course at a registered uni. It doesn't depend on household income.
- The loan gets paid directly to the university every year.

Give yourself time to apply for loans and plan how you're going to fund your studies.

Maintenance loans

- Maintenance loans are means-tested — the amount you get will depend on your circumstances.
- One way it's measured is by household income. You can get more money if your household income is lower.
- The amount you can claim depends on whether you're from England, Wales, Northern Ireland or Scotland.
- The amount also depends on whether you're living at home, away from home, or in London while you study.
- You may be entitled to more financial support if you're an independent student (see p.12).

 ## Important and Incredibly Fun Questions About Repaying Student Loans

You can find more information on how student loans work on the Student Finance website.

How and when will my loans be paid back?

- Repayments are based on how much you earn, not how much you borrow. They work like a tax.
- You won't start repayments until your salary goes above a certain threshold — this is different in each country in the UK and can change yearly. 9% of your income that's above this threshold will be taken automatically from your wages.
- Furthermore, for full-time students, repayments don't start until the April after graduation, even if they're earning above the threshold. For part-time students, repayments don't start until four years after the start of their course or the April after graduation (whichever is first).

Will my loans have interest on them?

- Your loans start earning interest as soon as you receive the first instalment. They will continue to gain interest until they've been repaid or cancelled.

 ### How long will I be repaying the loans?

- After 30 years, if you have any remaining student debt (which most people will), then the balance is wiped out and you won't have to repay any more money on your loans.
- Student debt doesn't affect your credit score, and so won't stop you getting a mortgage.

Financial Support

There are other types of financial support that can be awarded to students, such as grants, bursaries and scholarships. These are useful options if you're eligible for them because you don't have to pay them back.

Student Finance **Offers Some Grants**

Disabled Students' Allowance

- If you have a <u>long-term health condition</u>, a <u>mental health condition</u>, a <u>learning difficulty</u> or a <u>registered disability</u>, you could be entitled to this allowance.

- It can be put towards <u>support workers</u> and <u>specialist equipment</u> as well as your <u>general allowance</u>.

Support for Parents

- <u>Full-time students with children</u> might be entitled to the <u>Childcare Grant</u> or the <u>Parents' Learning Allowance</u>.

Support for People with Adult Dependants

- <u>Full-time students</u> with an <u>adult who depends on them financially</u> might be eligible for the <u>Adult Dependants' Grant</u>.

There Are Other Funding Opportunities

- Universities might offer a <u>fee waiver</u> (a tuition fee discount) or <u>bursary</u> for students from lower-income families.

- They might also offer <u>scholarships</u> on the basis of <u>academic achievement</u>, your <u>degree subject</u>, or <u>where you're from</u>.

- Most students do <u>part-time work</u> alongside their degree or find work <u>during the summer</u> if their course takes up too much of their time. It's great for your bank balance and for enhancing your CV.

Employer Support

University Support

Erasmus Grants

Part-time Work

- Some <u>companies</u> offer <u>bursaries</u> and <u>scholarships</u> to support people through their studies. You usually need to <u>work for the employer</u> for a <u>minimum amount</u> of time after graduating.

- <u>Erasmus Grants</u> might be available for students who <u>work or study in Europe</u> as part of their degree, to help with living costs while they're abroad.

Research your options to keep your finances shipshape...

If you're worried about whether you can afford university, you're in the same boat as a lot of other people. It's a good idea to ask someone at your school or college for advice if you need help understanding funding options.

Applying to Student Finance

If you do apply for Student Finance, you'll have to tackle it separately to your UCAS application. Luckily, two applications mean you get to have twice the fun. These are the basics of applying to Student Finance.

Each Country in the UK Has a Different Student Finance Company

1) You need to <u>apply directly</u> to the organisation <u>depending on where you live</u> in the UK. They're all called <u>Student Finance</u>, <u>apart from Scotland's</u> which is called the <u>Student Awards Agency Scotland</u>.

2) Applications normally open sometime <u>after the UCAS deadline</u> in January, but make sure you <u>check</u>.

3) To guarantee you'll be paid when your <u>course starts</u>, you need to apply in the <u>spring before it begins</u> — you can apply <u>online</u> or by <u>post</u>.

4) You can apply for student finance <u>before</u> you have a <u>confirmed university place</u>. Fill out your application based on where you're <u>most likely to study</u> and update it as soon as possible if it changes.

Sadie found it more difficult than she expected to open an account at the bank.

What You Need to Apply

- A working <u>email address</u>
- A <u>bank account</u> registered in your name
- Your <u>National Insurance Number</u>
- Details of your chosen <u>university</u> and <u>course</u>
- A <u>valid UK passport</u> — if you don't have one, you'll need an <u>original birth or adoption certificate</u> instead
- Your <u>parents' or guardians' details</u> (if you want them to support your application)

Make sure you keep your Student Finance application up to date with any changes once you've submitted it.

You Might Need to Supply More Information

1) If your <u>parents or guardians</u> choose to <u>support your application</u>, they'll need to send details about their <u>household income</u> — it might make you <u>eligible</u> for <u>more financial support</u>.

2) You can apply to be <u>assessed differently</u> if you're an <u>independent student</u>, e.g. if you're <u>over 25</u>, if you've <u>been in care</u>, or if you're an <u>estranged student</u> (not in contact with family). This means your maintenance allowance <u>won't depend</u> on your parents' income, but you might need to provide evidence of your personal or financial situation.

3) If you apply for <u>extra support</u> (e.g. Disabled Students' Allowance), you might need to send <u>supporting evidence</u> or attend a <u>Study Needs Assessment</u>.

Rodrigo was determined to have plenty of evidence ready for his Student Finance application.

For some reason, they weren't interested in my extra information about snails...

Before you apply for student finance, make sure that you have all the documents you need to apply and read the guidelines on the website carefully. Your application will be easier to process if there aren't any mistakes in it.

Support Options to Avoid

In the making of this book, we conducted thorough, painstaking (and at times painful) research into ways of funding a university degree. These are the ways which, from our experience, we wouldn't recommend...

 Selling £1 Coins at Half Price

We ran out of stock within thirty minutes — our mistake was clearly not having more coins to sell.

 Inventing a New Colour of Paint

Thinking about this idea for too long made our heads hurt.

Opening a Jumper Shop in the Desert

It turns out camels and snakes are more into caps and sunglasses.

Running a Sloth Walking Service

We sent one of the editors out when we started making the book and they still haven't come back.

Looking for Sunken Treasure

This one comes from a friend. (We haven't spoken since — something about an incident with a shark.)

Depositing Chocolate Coins into a Bank

It's apparently a weak currency that's liable to melt.

Wishing for Money using a Cursed Monkey's Paw

For legal reasons we're not allowed to comment further (RIP Colin).

Using a Metal Detector on the Beach

We discovered an ancient coin, the remains of a forgotten civilisation and a lost play by Shakespeare, but no money — such a waste of time.

These ideas are more useless than glow in the dark curtains...

We went through a lot during this research — we visited unusual places, failed in many business ventures and met a whole bunch of new people who think we're financially naive. But remember, we did it so you don't have to.

Introduction to UCAS

UCAS stands for the Universities and Colleges Admissions Service. No wonder it gets shortened, really. UCAS not only handles university applications, it also provides support to applicants throughout the process.

You Apply to University Through UCAS

1) If you're applying to <u>study full-time</u> at a <u>UK university</u>, you'll use UCAS to submit your application.

2) The great thing about UCAS is that rather than having to send a separate application to each of your chosen universities, you only need to <u>complete one application</u> and UCAS does the rest.

3) Applications open in <u>late May</u> and are done through the <u>UCAS website</u> — there's more about how to fill in your application on <u>pages 36-43</u>.

4) You can submit your application from <u>early September</u>, but as long as you submit it <u>before the deadline</u>, you'll have just as equal a chance of being considered as everyone else.

5) <u>Deadlines</u> for when you need to submit your application by <u>vary</u> — some of the main dates are on the board to the right. Your <u>school or college</u> might set its <u>own deadline</u>, so check with them to find out whether they do.

DEADLINES

15th October —
If you're applying to Oxford or Cambridge, or to courses such as medicine, dentistry, veterinary medicine / science.

15th January —
The deadline for most other universities and courses.

> There's an <u>administration fee</u> to pay when you submit your UCAS application — this is usually <u>around £25</u>. Some schools and colleges <u>pay this</u> for you.

You can keep a track of the deadlines you need on p.36.

You Can Apply for Five Courses

1) University admissions are <u>competitive</u>, so applying for a number of courses <u>improves your chance</u> of getting an offer.

2) You get up to <u>five choices</u>, but you can submit your application with fewer. If you choose to <u>add more choices later</u>, you add them using <u>UCAS Track</u> (the online system which tracks your application).

3) UCAS sends the <u>same application</u> to each of your five choices — try to <u>apply for similar courses</u> so that your application makes sense for all of them.

Kyle wished he'd waited until the end of dinner to tell his date that there would only be one course.

Some Exceptions

- If you're applying for <u>medical courses</u>, you can only choose <u>four</u> of these. You can also add a <u>fifth course</u> that's <u>not a medical course</u> (see p.22).

- If you want to study at <u>Oxford or Cambridge</u>, you can <u>only</u> apply to <u>one course at either university</u>.

For more on how to pick a course, see pages 20-21.

Introduction to UCAS

You Need a Reference to Support Your Application

1) The reference is a <u>statement written by someone else</u> to support your application. It's <u>important</u> because it's an <u>extra chance</u> to prove your <u>suitability to study at university</u>.

2) It's usually <u>written by a tutor</u> at your school or college, but there are <u>other options</u> for students applying independently (see p.79).

3) The reference is meant to <u>reflect your performance</u> across all subjects, so your referee might consult other tutors before writing it.

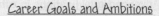
Conservatoires ask for two references — one academic and one practical reference.

Your Reference Might Include:

Academic Ability and Performance

This includes your <u>post-16 achievements</u>, <u>predicted grades</u> and the <u>quality</u> of your work.

Career Goals and Ambitions

These help show your <u>motivation</u> and <u>commitment</u> to your chosen subject area.

Work Ethic, Attitude and Key Skills

The reference might discuss the way you <u>approach</u> studying your current subjects and how your <u>skills prepare</u> you <u>for university study</u>.

Interest in the Subject

They could talk about the <u>different ways</u> that you show interest in your subject <u>in school</u> and <u>outside your classes</u>.

Extra-Curricular Activities and Work Experience

This includes things like if you've gained <u>leadership skills</u> from <u>mentoring</u> and how this will help you with your <u>degree</u>.

Talk to Your Referee About the Reference

1) Some tutors have <u>lots of references</u> to write. If you chat to them about it beforehand, they'll have a better idea of <u>what to include</u> for you personally.

2) If there are any <u>personal circumstances</u> which have affected your studies (e.g. <u>bereavement</u> or <u>illness</u>), your tutor can mention these in your reference <u>with your permission</u>. This gives universities <u>useful context</u> when they're considering your application.

Hercules hoped that his reference would be an accurate reflection of his character.

My referee did a really good job of talking about my football skills...

The reference is really just another opportunity to show that you're an ideal candidate for the courses you're applying for. Find out who'll be writing your reference early on and make sure they know what your goals are.

How Universities Compare Applications

Knowing how universities make their decisions can help you choose where and how to apply. Luckily for you, they don't just pick names out of a hat. Here are some of the main criteria they use.

QUALIFICATIONS AND GRADES

- Entry requirements are the conditions that universities ask you to meet to study the course — this often means achieving certain grades or a certain UCAS Tariff Points total.
- Universities use your GCSEs and predicted A-Level grades (or equivalent) to see how likely it is that you'll be able to meet the entry requirements before they make you an offer.
- If you want to see how many UCAS Tariff Points your grades are worth, you can use the Tariff Points Calculator on the UCAS website to find out.
- Advanced qualifications in other areas, such as music, drama, dance and sport, can also be worth UCAS Tariff Points. You need to add these to your application before you submit it.
- Make sure you check whether your chosen universities will accept each of your qualifications before you apply to them.

The UCAS Tariff Points system attaches points to different post-16 qualifications to measure their value.

A-Level Grade	UCAS Tariff Points
A*	56
A	48
B	40
C	32
D	24

YOUR PASSION

- Universities want to know that you're passionate about the subject you're applying to study. They'll be looking for people who show an interest in the subject outside the classroom, such as people who do further reading, take extra courses or volunteer.
- Admissions tutors will look for evidence of this in your personal statement and reference, which is part of the reason they're both such important aspects of your application.
- You can find more about how to stand out from the crowd in your application on p.48-49.

EXTRA REQUIREMENTS

Once you've submitted your UCAS application, some universities will contact you about further requirements you need to meet before they consider offering you a place. These can include:

- Taking an admissions test (e.g. for medicine or law)
- Submitting written work (e.g. English Literature essays)
- Attending an interview or audition

Universities and admissions officers use these extra requirements to decide between candidates for highly competitive courses.

Suki had spent so long comparing applications that she'd gained the power to make them float.

I've always thought my passion for bad jokes was beyond compare...

Researching the entry requirements for a course is really important. Not only will it help you decide where to apply, but it'll mean you can prepare for any tests or other additional requirements that you'll need to meet.

How Universities Compare Applications

I asked the best admissions officers (that I could find) what they look for when considering applications. It should be noted that some of these responses have been edited slightly — just a smidge *cough*...

John Beats

I only ever consider giving an applicant an offer if their personal statement is written in a poetic form. Rhyming couplets will definitely grab my attention, but if you have the ability to write in trochaic tetrameter then I'll almost certainly want you at my university. Don't bother with this half-rhyme nonsense though.

Michelleangela

I want applicants to paint a picture of themselves — literally. Show me your soul through watercolour, show me your passion through fingerpaint, show me your wonderful summer holiday through a selfie. To indicate that you've done extra research, draw a portrait of me too — I'll put it up on my fridge.

Miss Heard

A student's voice is important, so I gravitate towards applicants that include a dramatic reading of their personal statement. I look for tense pauses, different accents for each paragraph and inventive impressions (my favourite being 'a parrot singing a sea shanty').

Cody Breaker

i like it when Students includE hidden codes iN their applications. it can Demonstrate that they're able To think in a logicAl way and it Can make an applicatiOn really memorable. yeah, that'S what i like...

It doesn't come across, but that Cody is obsessed with Mexican food...

It was only as I was editing these testimonials that I realised I may not have found the best set of admissions officers to ask. It's probably safer if you save the dramatic readings of your application for an open mic night.

Different Types of Courses

There are plenty of different things to consider when you're choosing a course and a university. The next few pages are packed with lots of helpful information on how to go about making both of those decisions.

You Can Choose Your Course or Your University First

1) There's no correct order to pick your course and university in.

2) You could find a course that you feel passionate about and then see whether the university is the right place for you.

3) Or, if there's a place that you'd like to live, you could start by looking at nearby universities and seeing if they do a course that interests you.

4) You might have to make some compromises between your course and your university. For example, a course with perfect modules may be at a university that is too far away. If something like this happens, you'll have to decide if a great course or a great university is more important to you.

Maxine loved snowy places, but in hindsight, she had compromised too much on the quality of her catering degree.

There Are Different Types of Undergraduate Course

Most undergraduate courses are bachelor's degrees, for example a Bachelor of Arts (BA) or Bachelor of Science (BSc) degree, which normally last three or four years. But there are some variations:

A degree with 'Hons' after it is an honours degree. These degrees show that the person has attained a specific level of study. Many bachelor's degrees come with honours.

Single honours degrees are the most common type of bachelor's degree. They focus on studying one subject area.

A major / minor bachelor's degree lets you study two or more subjects that are weighted unequally as part of the same degree.

Joint / Combined honours degrees are a type of bachelor's degree which allow you to study two or more subjects equally as part of the same degree.

A foundation year is an extra year of study that leads into a full degree programme. It's a great option if you don't have the right grades or subjects to get onto the course directly.

Integrated Master's degrees are undergraduate courses that include an extra year of postgraduate-level study and award both a bachelor's and a master's degree. They're more common in sciences and engineering.

Foundation degrees are usually two-year courses that have lower entry requirements than bachelor's degrees. They're great options for students who don't want to commit to three years of study.

Different Types of Courses

You Can Study Full-Time or Part-Time

1) <u>Full-time courses</u> usually take <u>three or four years</u> to complete. The <u>pace</u> of full-time study is <u>more intensive</u> because you're expected to make the course your <u>biggest commitment</u>.

   • Full-time study often makes it easier to become more <u>immersed</u> in your <u>subject</u> and the <u>university experience</u> because it's your main focus.

   • Studying full-time lets you get your degree <u>as soon as possible</u> and allows you to move on to <u>further study</u> or <u>get a job</u> related to your qualification sooner.

   • <u>Some courses</u>, like <u>medicine</u>, can <u>only be studied full-time</u>.

2) <u>Part-time courses</u> offer <u>more flexibility</u>. You'll study the <u>same content</u> as a full-time student, but <u>over a longer period of time</u> (generally five or more years).

   • Part-time study lets you <u>balance your degree with other commitments</u>, e.g. work or family life.

   • The <u>slower pace</u> of the course can be <u>helpful</u> for students whose circumstances make <u>full-time</u> study more <u>difficult</u>, e.g. because of specific health conditions.

   • Part-time courses <u>aren't available</u> at <u>every university</u> or for <u>every course</u>.

There Are Other Options Available

Some undergraduate courses can be <u>adapted</u> to give you <u>extra opportunities</u> or <u>more flexibility</u> while you study — take a look at these options:

Degrees with a <u>sandwich year</u> include an <u>extra year</u> which is spent doing something related to the course away from the university. This could be <u>studying or working abroad</u>, or <u>working in industry</u> elsewhere in the UK. They are a great opportunity to gain <u>more experience</u> before graduating.

Jordan quite liked the sound of a degree with a sandwich year.

Distance learning allows you to study your degree <u>anywhere</u> and complete it at <u>your own pace</u> (full-time or part-time). <u>The Open University</u> is one of the main course providers for distance learning, but it's available at other unis as well. Course content is usually <u>accessed online</u> and there are sometimes <u>residential workshops</u>. You <u>apply directly to the university</u>.

<u>Accelerated degrees</u> last for <u>two years</u> and are only offered by a <u>limited number of universities</u>. They're <u>more intensive</u>, but <u>can be cheaper</u> over the two years — while the annual tuition fees might be more expensive, you'll save on living costs.

You don't have to follow the crowd, of course...

A full-time single honours degree might be the most popular type of course, but that doesn't mean it's right for everyone — think about your circumstances and how long you want to spend studying before you make a decision.

How to Choose a Course

One of the most important decisions you'll make when applying to university is choosing a course. It can take a bit of time to figure out what you want to study, so start thinking about it as soon as possible.

Don't Panic If You Don't Know What to Study

1) Look at the <u>subjects you currently study</u> and think about whether you'd like to <u>continue studying</u> any of them at university.

2) <u>Consider subjects</u> that you <u>haven't studied before</u>. There's so much choice at university that it's a <u>great time</u> to try <u>something new</u> — you could learn a new language, or study a subject like engineering, gender studies or criminology.

3) Think about your <u>interests</u>, <u>skills</u>, and what you might <u>enjoy</u>. You'll study your subject for a while, so enjoyment is important.

4) Try using the <u>UCAS</u> website's <u>course search</u> feature to get some ideas — you can enter keywords (e.g. 'animals') and see what comes up.

5) Consider doing a <u>free online course</u> in the subject to see if you enjoy it.

6) If you find yourself wanting to study <u>more than one subject</u>, try researching <u>joint</u>, <u>combined</u> or <u>major / minor</u> degrees (see p.18).

> Try asking a careers advisor for some suggestions of subjects or courses that might suit you.

Tess was starting to regret picking Conflict Studies as her degree subject.

> Look at the kind of <u>entry requirements</u> and <u>job prospects</u> there are for the subjects you're interested in — work out whether these are <u>suitable</u> for your <u>ability</u> and <u>goals</u>.

> Use the space below to jot down any thoughts you have.

> You could draw a mind map, write a list, or do whatever works best for you. Think about the subjects and areas you might want to research more.

How to Choose a Course

Look at Different Courses to Find the Right One for You

Courses with the same name can vary quite a lot. For example, an English Literature course at one university might focus on classical literature, while another might focus on modern literature and film. Think about the following things when deciding how to narrow down your search:

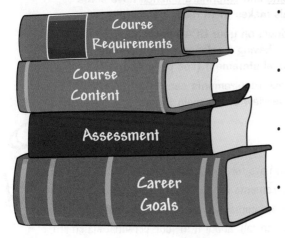

- Look at whether the entry requirements are achievable. Give yourself options — find one course with requirements below your predicted grades and another exceeding them.

- Choose courses that have modules and specialities you're interested in. You could choose a more varied course if you don't know what you want to specialise in yet.

- Some courses are mainly assessed by exams, while others put more emphasis on coursework. Play to your strengths so that you have the best chance to excel.

- Look at what previous students do now. Check if the course includes any work experience or work-related modules that would help with your career goals.

Take Time to Do Your Research

The key to choosing the courses that are right for you is leaving plenty of time for research and making use of all the resources available to you. Here's a handy mind map of some useful places to look:

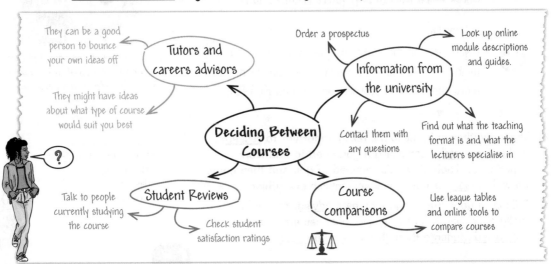

I won't subject you to any puns here, I promise...

You might not know what course you want to study just yet, but try and see the amount of choice as a bonus. If you do your research properly, you'll end up studying a degree course that you love for the next few years.

Applying for Medical Courses

If you want to be a doctor, a dentist or a vet, this page is for you. The application process for medical courses differs to that of other courses — this page will give you an overview of the main differences.

Medical Courses Are Competitive

1) Courses like medicine, dentistry, veterinary medicine and veterinary science have some of the highest number of applicants per place. This makes them really competitive.

2) You can only put four of these types of courses down on your UCAS application. Luckily, you can still add a different fifth course — having a science-related course is best because it will still link well with your personal statement (see page 45).

3) These courses also have extra requirements — these requirements can differ between universities and courses, but here's an overview of the main three:

Work experience

Find out what type of experience you need to have for each course and, if you haven't already, organise some work experience. Types of placements include volunteering at a care home, shadowing a GP, or helping on a farm or at an animal sanctuary. Make a note of what you learn from this work experience so that you can talk about it in your personal statement.

Admissions tests

The two main tests used for medical courses are the BMAT and the UCAT. There's more about these on p.69. Check which tests (if any) you're required to sit.

Interviews

If you meet all the other entry requirements, you might get asked to an interview. You can learn more about how to prepare for them on p.64-67.

Ling was sure all the animal photos she'd posted on social media would count as veterinary work experience.

4) These requirements mean it's really important to research and prepare early, especially if you need to find work experience. Look at what's required of you and then come up with a plan for how you'll accomplish everything.

5) Talking to your tutors and a careers advisor can be a really good way to get advice — chances are, they've supported students through the same process in the past.

Remember that these courses also have an earlier deadline — see page 14.

With some early preparation, it's all going tibia fine...

You'll give yourself the best chance of being accepted onto one of these courses if you research the extra entry requirements and make sure that you meet them all. It's important to be prepared for the tests and interviews too.

How to Choose a University

Choosing a university is like choosing a cake — you need to think hard about what matters the most to you so that you can get the most enjoyable and rewarding cake. I mean university. Yes, definitely university...

There Are Lots Of Criteria to Consider

The **size** of the university — a large university will likely have more resources and facilities, whereas a smaller one may have a stronger and more tight-knit community.

Whether you want a **campus** or **non-campus** university — everything is conveniently located on campuses, but some students may find themselves more likely to explore the town or city at a non-campus university.

Whether to choose a university with a **collegiate system** — colleges can create smaller communities, making it easier to meet people and take part in activities.

Whether you can still do your **hobbies** — e.g. surfers may look at universities near the coast, and skiers might consider universities near ski slopes.

The **surroundings** — you'll be there for a long time, so don't settle for the middle of a busy city if you'd rather be somewhere more rural.

Whether the university is **suitable for your needs** — e.g. are the buildings easily accessible, are there good disability and mental health services, etc.

Yorkshire and the Dales

Whether the university has **specialised facilities** — e.g. some universities are renowned for their great sports facilities.

The **distance from home** — some students want a fresh start in a new place, but others choose to live with their parents to save money. You should also consider how easy and expensive it'll be to get home.

The **cost of living** — accommodation in some major cities, such as London, is typically more expensive than in other places.

How the university **compares to others** — you could check student satisfaction or graduate employment ratings.

The **cost of tuition** — some universities may be slightly cheaper than others or offer extra financial support.

How to Choose a University

There Are Different Ways to Look For Universities

1) There's <u>not one perfect way</u> to start your <u>search for a university</u>.

2) If you <u>know where</u> you want to live, e.g. because you're planning to live at home, then you could start by seeing if there are any <u>nearby universities</u> that interest you.

3) If you know there's a <u>course</u> that <u>excites you</u> at a certain university, then you can research this university in more depth to see if its <u>other qualities</u> appeal to you.

Nick looked for a university as close to home as possible.

There Are Plenty of Places to Find Information

University websites and social media

- <u>Websites</u> can offer <u>important facts</u>, such as <u>course information</u>, <u>accommodation costs</u> and where to find the <u>best fajitas</u> on campus. Universities are trying to <u>attract students</u> though, so they will likely shy away from negative points.

- A university's <u>social media</u> presence can give you a feel for the type of <u>community</u> and <u>events</u> they have.

University fairs and open days

- At fairs, you can pick up <u>university prospectuses</u> and <u>speak to people</u> from the universities <u>face-to-face</u>. Fairs are a good way to see what universities have to offer, but also what they want from applicants.

- Going to an <u>open day</u> can help you get an <u>impression</u> of <u>what life is like</u> at the university (see <u>pages 32-33</u>).

Ranking tables

- <u>University league tables</u> are great for getting a <u>general feel</u> of how good a university is.

- Different sources (e.g. The Complete University Guide and The Guardian) rank on different criteria. Some look at <u>student satisfaction</u>, while others look at the <u>quality of teaching</u>.

Students and alumni

- <u>Talking to students</u> can give you <u>feedback</u> from someone who has <u>made the choice</u> you're trying to make. They can tell you <u>what's great</u>, but also warn you about <u>potential downsides</u>.

- You can usually speak to students at <u>open days</u>, but you can also find <u>student groups online</u>.

Admissions officers

- <u>Contacting a university</u> directly is a great way of getting <u>answers</u> to questions that you <u>can't find elsewhere</u> (except maybe "Why do we dream?").

My friend and I are scout leaders — it's why we chose campus universities...

If you're torn between universities, try scoring each one against the factors on page 23. This might help you split the hairs on which university you prefer (it's also a great excuse to create a spreadsheet, which is always a win).

Choosing a University Abroad

If the idea of studying in the rain-plagued UK fills you with ghoulish dread, then this page on choosing a university abroad will liven you up. Here's what you need to know about applying somewhere further afield.

Studying Abroad Has Some Differences

Some universities will have lectures and seminars in the **native language**, so you might want to find courses that are **delivered in English**. You may also have to pass a **language test**.

You **won't use UCAS** to apply to universities abroad — you'll either **apply directly** to the **university** or use a **different admissions service**. **Deadlines** will also **differ** from UK applications, so research these **early**.

It's certainly a different atmosphere to home...

It can be **harder to make friends** abroad, so look at countries and universities that have **good services** and **societies** for **international students**.

Some countries require you to have a **visa** to work or study there. Check **how early** you need to **apply** for a visa.

If you want to **travel** while you're abroad, consider where you want to visit and look at **universities** that are **nearby**.

Getting Funding to Study Abroad can be Tricky

1) Tuition fees vary in each country. Some fees are higher than in the UK, while some countries have no tuition fees at all.

2) It's also worth noting that some countries have a higher cost of living than the UK. You'll need to weigh this up alongside tuition fees when determining how much studying abroad may cost you.

3) You won't be eligible for loans through Student Finance (see pages 10-12) if you do your entire degree abroad.

4) Research other financial support — some UK organisations and foreign universities offer scholarships, grants and loans to UK students studying abroad, but these are likely to be competitive.

5) You might be able to get a part-time job while studying abroad. You'll need to check if you're allowed to work in your chosen country and if there's a limit on the number of hours you can do.

Laura placed all her hopes in the money tree she bought from the not-at-all-suspicious internet seller.

If you're struggling to get funds, you could look at UK universities that offer opportunities to study abroad as part of their course. This would allow you to apply for loans and grants from Student Finance.

Choosing a Russell Group University

The Russell Group universities, including Oxford and Cambridge, are renowned across the world. You've probably seen their names in all sorts of places — glossy magazines, merchandised tea towels, road signs...

Russell Group Universities Offer Brilliant Teaching

1) Russell Group universities pride themselves on being high-quality, research-focused institutions. They are regarded as having an excellent standard of teaching and for providing the very best education.

2) Students from Russell Group universities are highly sought after by employers and, because of their reputation, courses at these universities tend to have higher entry requirements and are more competitive.

Russell loved listening to his favourite group.

3) However, this doesn't mean that all the top courses are at Russell Group universities or that you're guaranteed the best university experience at one. There are universities like the University of St Andrews and Lancaster University that aren't in the Russell Group, but which often outrank Russell Group universities in the league tables. The best courses for some subjects may also be outside of this group.

4) As always, it's about finding the right fit for you — a top student with a CV full of relevant skills from another university can be just as appealing to employers.

Oxford and Cambridge Seek the Very Best Students

Oxford and Cambridge (sometimes nicknamed Oxbridge) are even more competitive, but they are also two of the finest universities about. Take a look inside the mind of our Oxbridge guru for some information.

You can't apply to both Oxford and Cambridge in the same year. They're quite similar, so think about which course and city would suit you best too.

The UCAS deadline for Oxbridge is earlier (15th October), so you need to prepare your application early.

The learning style is more personal — you'll have tutorials with just one or two other students.

There's a big workload. You'll prepare an essay or other work for each tutorial — you might have these twice a week.

You'll likely have to go for an interview, take additional tests and send in samples of work as part of your application (see pages 64-69).

Each university is made up of colleges. These are small communities where you live and work while still belonging to a large institution. You can apply to a specific college or make an open application.

Both cities are beautiful to their very core...

Choosing a Conservatoire

A conservatoire isn't a house extension that's pleasant to sit in during the summer — it's an institution that specialises in the performing arts and can offer courses in music, dance, theatre, production and circus arts.

Conservatoires Differ to Universities

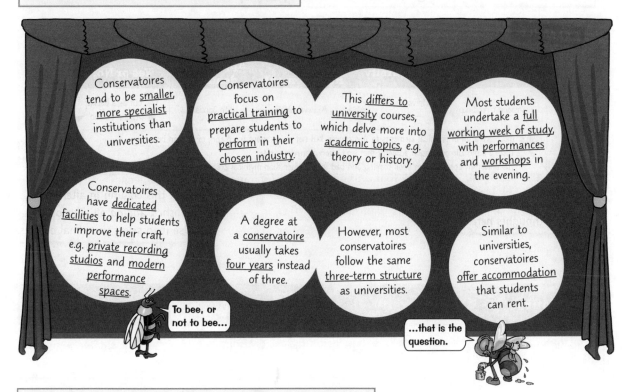

Application Processes For Conservatoires Vary

1) You can apply to some conservatoires through UCAS Conservatoires — this is like the UCAS Apply service, but just for conservatoires. For other conservatoires, you'll have to apply directly. Research what you need to do for each conservatoire you're interested in.

2) In the 2020 intake, you could apply to six conservatoires through UCAS Conservatoires. You could also apply to five undergraduate courses (e.g. music and drama) at university through the normal UCAS system.

3) Different types of course have different UCAS Conservatoire deadlines:

> Music courses need to be applied for by early October.

> Most dance, drama and musical theatre courses have a deadline in mid-January.

UCAS may be making changes to conservatoire applications after the 2020 intake. Check the UCAS website for updated information.

4) You'll have to take part in an audition or an interview after submitting your application (see page 68).

Break a leg if you apply to a conservatoire — you'll get yourself a free cast...

The practical side of performing arts isn't for everyone, so make sure you're confident it's the right thing for you.

Course and University Options

Here are a couple of pages for you to jot down some information about the options you're considering. You can then rate and eliminate them until only the best remain — it's like a really wild reality TV show...

Summarise Your Thoughts About Each Option

EXAMPLE:

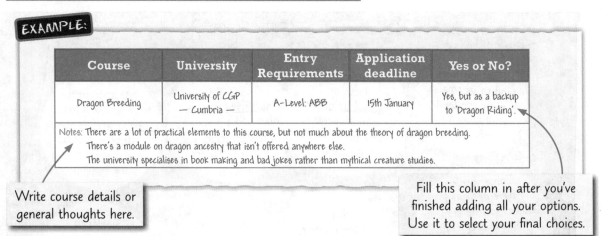

Course	University	Entry Requirements	Application deadline	Yes or No?
Dragon Breeding	University of CGP — Cumbria —	A-Level: ABB	15th January	Yes, but as a backup to 'Dragon Riding'.

Notes: There are a lot of practical elements to this course, but not much about the theory of dragon breeding.
There's a module on dragon ancestry that isn't offered anywhere else.
The university specialises in book making and bad jokes rather than mythical creature studies.

Write course details or general thoughts here.

Fill this column in after you've finished adding all your options. Use it to select your final choices.

Course	University	Entry Requirements	Application deadline	Yes or No?

Notes:

Notes:

Course and University Options

Course	University	Entry Requirements	Application deadline	Yes or No?

Notes:

Notes:

Notes:

Notes:

Course and University Options

Course	University	Entry Requirements	Application deadline	Yes or No?

Notes:

Notes:

Notes:

Notes:

Course and University Options

Course	University	Entry Requirements	Application deadline	Yes or No?
Notes:				
Notes:				
Notes:				
Notes:				

Yes or no, left or right, ketchup or barbecue sauce — all important decisions...

I always use a table to write down information when I need to consider all of my options and make a decision. It's really useful — the only downside is that my friends have stopped inviting me over for dinner parties...

Open Days

An open day can help you to picture what living and studying somewhere might be like before you apply.

Open Days Make Universities Feel More Personal

1) It's hard to get a sense of whether a university is right for you just from a <u>website</u> or <u>prospectus</u>.

2) Open days include <u>talks and tours</u> you can attend to give you a better idea:

- <u>Course talks</u> will give you a greater insight into what and how things are taught at the university.
- <u>Student life talks</u> cover a range of topics, such as support services, student societies and study abroad opportunities. They're useful for getting a better sense of what life outside your course might be like.
- <u>Tours of the university</u> are usually run by current students — it's a chance to learn about the facilities from someone who uses them.

Alice got the feeling the tour guide didn't know the way to the library.

3) You can often <u>ask</u> current students and course tutors <u>questions</u> about the university or course.

4) There might be a chance to <u>view accommodation</u> — this can help you to decide between <u>different types of accommodation</u> (e.g. ensuite or shared bathroom) and <u>different catering options</u>. You can also can get an idea of the distance to your lecture buildings and <u>decide whether</u> you'd be <u>happy living there</u>.

5) You should research open day dates <u>early</u> — some universities run open days <u>before the academic year</u> begins.

You can find the dates of open days on a university's website or by using the UCAS events search feature.

Plan Your Day Before You Arrive

1) If there are <u>events</u> that interest you (e.g. <u>talks</u> or <u>taster sessions</u>), check whether you need to <u>book in advance</u>.

2) <u>Plan your day</u> carefully, factoring in talks you've booked and <u>ensuring you have time</u> to see <u>departments</u> and other places nearby (e.g. <u>sports facilities</u> or <u>places to eat</u>).

3) See if a <u>friend</u> or <u>family member</u> will go with you. Having a <u>second opinion</u> can be <u>helpful</u>.

4) Plan <u>how you'll get there</u> — some universities offer <u>car parking</u>, but it might be easier to use <u>public transport</u>. If you want to <u>stay overnight</u> to get a better feel for the area, take this into account when planning your travel.

5) If you might need any <u>extra provisions</u> made (e.g. <u>mobility</u> or <u>accessibility</u>), let the university know ahead of time so they can put <u>appropriate measures</u> in place.

6) Make a <u>list of questions</u> (and take it with you) so you don't forget to ask anything you want to. Also <u>bring a pen</u> and <u>paper</u> so you can <u>make notes</u>.

Open Day To-Do List

- ☐ Plan which <u>tours</u>, <u>talks</u> and <u>departments</u> you want to see
- ☐ <u>Book</u> places on useful <u>talks</u>
- ☐ Plan <u>travel arrangements</u>
- ☐ Make a <u>list of questions</u>
- ☐ Bring a <u>pen and paper</u> so you can make <u>notes</u>

Open Days

Go to As Many Open Days As You Can

1) It's generally a <u>good idea</u> to go to <u>as many</u> open days <u>as possible</u>, especially if you're <u>deciding between</u> a number of <u>different universities</u>.

2) However, there is <u>no correct number</u> of open days you should attend. Some people only go to <u>one or two</u>, while others go to <u>more than ten</u>. If you can, try to visit the universities that you plan to <u>apply</u> to or <u>accept an offer</u> from.

3) The most important thing is that you <u>visit as many</u> universities <u>as you need</u> to be <u>happy</u> about your choices.

The gang believed that if they laughed hard enough, they could hide the regret of not attending any open days.

Open Day Bursaries

<u>Travelling</u> the country for open days can get <u>expensive</u>, but some universities offer help, e.g. <u>bursaries</u>, <u>free accommodation</u>, <u>discounted travel</u>, etc. Look at the <u>university's website</u> to see what they offer.

Sometimes You Might Not Make It to an Open Day

If you're <u>unable to attend</u> a university's open day, you can get a feel for the university in <u>other ways</u>.

- Some universities offer <u>virtual tours</u> that you can access online. These tours are done using <u>interactive videos and images</u>. They can give you a glimpse of what the <u>university's facilities</u> are like from the comfort of your own <u>home</u>.

- <u>Podcasts</u> are also sometimes available. These often contain <u>recordings of talks</u> from the open day, so you can <u>get the information</u> even if you <u>didn't attend</u>.

- You can try <u>visiting</u> on a <u>different day</u>. Some universities have <u>multiple open days</u>, but you could also just <u>visit</u> or <u>stay in the area</u> for a weekend if it has a course you really like.

- If you have any burning questions about the course, you can <u>contact the university</u> — they might be able to get an answer from a <u>lecturer</u> in the <u>department</u>.

Some universities also run open days for students who they've given an offer to (see page 72).

I'm open to days, but night time terrifies me...

Try not to feel disheartened if you attend an open day and you don't like the university or the course. See it as a positive — it's better to know it isn't for you now than when you've already committed and you're stuck there.

Open Days

More write-in pages — this time they're for all your thoughts about the open days you attend. These can be positive thoughts, negative thoughts, or any other thoughts that spring to mind.

Summarise Your Thoughts After Each Open Day

EXAMPLE:

Course	University	Open Day Date	Thoughts After the Day
Alien Invasion Studies	University of CGP	Saturday 28th October	Course tutor is open to field research. Only offers bouncy castles for accommodation. Impressive library filled with fantastic books.

Fill these in before the open day so you don't forget when it is.

Fill this in with your impressions of the course and university after you've been to the open day.

Course	University	Open Day Date	Thoughts After the Day

Choosing a Course and University

Open Days

Course	University	Open Day Date	Thoughts After the Day

These write-in pages are right on — people still say 'right on', right?...

The most important thing to note down on these pages is the date of each open day. If there are any that clash, check if the universities have alternative open days, or try to arrange a different day to visit one of the universities.

How to Fill in Your Application

Deadlines

Knowing deadlines is vital when applying to university. Luckily, there's space to jot them down right here...

There Are Different Deadlines You Need to Know

1) Find out when you can start filling in your application and when you need to have it completed by, — check whether there are any early deadlines for courses you're applying to as well (see page 14).

2) Once you start hearing back from universities, make a note of when you need to reply to offers by. The deadline can vary depending on when you get your application in and when you get all your responses — double-check this on UCAS Track.

3) Be aware of the opening and closing dates for services like UCAS Extra (see page 75), UCAS Clearing (see pages 76-77) or UCAS Adjustment (see page 78).

Dates to Find Out Now
- When UCAS Apply opens
- Deadline for Oxbridge and most medicine, veterinary medicine / science and dentistry courses (if relevant)
- Deadline for most undergraduate courses
- Deadlines set by your school or college

Dates to Find Out After Submitting Your Application
- Deadlines for responding to offers
- When UCAS Extra opens / closes
- When UCAS Clearing opens / closes
- When UCAS Adjustment opens / closes

Look on UCAS Track or ask your tutor to help you make sure you've got those all-important dates right.

Once you have your list of deadlines, put them in a calendar too — if you have a smartphone, set yourself reminders in advance so that you don't forget them.

Event	Date	Time (if applicable)

Making an Application Timetable

With how busy you'll be in the year leading up to university, the sooner you get your application sorted out the better you'll feel. The next few pages are for you to map out your game plan for the coming weeks...

Create a List of Tasks

1) Jot down a list of <u>things you need to do</u> before <u>sending</u> in your <u>application</u>, e.g write a personal statement, talk to your referee, etc.

2) Split these tasks into <u>manageable chunks</u> — consider <u>how long</u> you think they'll take, whether you need <u>anyone else's input</u>, and any <u>other commitments</u> you have planned.

> **Write Personal Statement**
> - Get ideas down
> - Write first draft
> - Leave time for numerous drafts
> - Get feedback

Add Your Deadlines and Tasks to the Timetable

1) Put any <u>deadlines</u> you're working towards into the <u>timetable</u> on pages 38-40.

2) <u>Add</u> your <u>tasks</u> to your <u>timetable</u>, giving yourself enough time to <u>finish</u> everything <u>well before</u> the <u>final deadline</u>.

3) <u>Don't worry</u> about filling the timetable out <u>all in one go</u>. Start off with a <u>general idea</u> and <u>then</u> work out the <u>specifics</u>.

EXAMPLE:

If your deadline is the 15th of January, your timetable for mid-October might look like this:

Day: Week:	Monday	Tuesday	Wednesday	Thursday	Friday	Weekend
9th–15th October		Edit current draft of personal statement		Give personal statement to tutor to read		Egg and spoon practice
16th–22nd October	Happy Birthday to me	Talk to tutor about my reference		Egg and spoon race		
23rd–29th October	Finish sections 5 and 6 of UCAS application			Re-read finished sections of UCAS application		Open day visit at CGP University

Split tasks into chunks

Add your commitments and activities

Leave plenty of time to get tasks done before your deadline

My, my, my, how the tables have turned — I mean, are going to be filled in...

Plan on submitting your application in advance of any deadlines. If you do it just before, something is bound to go wrong — your internet will go down, you'll spot an error in your personal statement, your dog will eat your laptop...

Application Timetable

Day: / Week:	Monday	Tuesday	Wednesday	Thursday	Friday	Weekend

Application Timetable

Day: / Week:	Monday	Tuesday	Wednesday	Thursday	Friday	Weekend

Application Timetable

Day: / Week:	Monday	Tuesday		Thursday	Friday	Weekend

Filling in Your Application

Now for the moment you've been waiting for — it's time to find out how to fill in your application. The next few pages will guide you through each of the sections and give you some tips about how to complete them.

Register on UCAS Apply

1) UCAS Apply is the <u>online system</u> you use to send your <u>UCAS application</u>.

2) When you <u>register</u>, you'll have to enter a few <u>personal details</u>, including your <u>name</u> and your school's <u>buzzword</u> (ask your tutor for this).

3) UCAS will generate a <u>username</u> for you, but you'll need to create your own <u>password</u>. You can use these to <u>sign in</u> to your UCAS Apply account and <u>work on</u> your application.

4) <u>You don't have to finish</u> your application in one go — you can <u>save each section</u> as you go along.

Fill in Your Personal Details

1) Most of this will be relatively straightforward — your <u>name</u>, <u>address</u>, <u>email address</u>, <u>nationality</u>, etc. <u>Some information</u> might <u>already</u> be filled in from when you <u>registered</u> on UCAS.

2) You'll have to fill out some <u>other information</u> too, including:

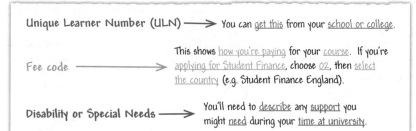

Unique Learner Number (ULN) ——▶ You can <u>get this</u> from your <u>school or college</u>.

Fee code ——▶ This shows <u>how you're paying</u> for your <u>course</u>. If you're <u>applying for Student Finance</u>, choose <u>02</u>, then <u>select the country</u> (e.g. Student Finance England).

Disability or Special Needs ——▶ You'll need to <u>describe</u> any <u>support</u> you might <u>need</u> during your <u>time at university</u>.

Ben was sure UCAS would love his PastaMaster@azmail.co.uk email address.

Add Additional Information

You'll be asked for information about things like your <u>ethnicity</u>, <u>religion</u> and <u>sexual orientation</u>.

UCAS collects this information for statistical purposes. If you'd rather not answer these questions, just click "I prefer not to say".

There's also space to fill out up to two <u>experiences</u> you've had that are <u>relevant</u> to your application (e.g. <u>summer schools</u> and <u>taster courses</u>).

You'll also be asked whether you've <u>been in public care</u>. If you have, you might be <u>eligible</u> for <u>financial and other support</u>.

Filling in Your Application

Say If You're Applying for Student Finance

1) If you entered the Student Finance <u>fee code</u> earlier in the application, you'll have to <u>tick a box</u> saying if you're <u>applying</u> for <u>student finance</u>.

2) If you tick '<u>yes</u>', you'll be asked if you'd like to <u>share your details</u> with Student Finance and be <u>notified</u> by UCAS when Student Finance <u>applications open</u>.

3) Remember that this <u>isn't the same thing</u> as applying for student finance — you've got to <u>apply</u> for your loan <u>through Student Finance</u> itself (see page 12).

Xuan was thrilled that Riku was around to help with her application.

Select Your Choices

You'll need to fill out the following information for <u>each of your course choices</u>:

The <u>course name</u> or <u>code</u>

The <u>course start date</u> (you select this from a list)

If you want to defer your place and your university is happy with this, set the start date for a year later.

The <u>university name</u> or <u>institution code</u> as well as the <u>campus code</u>

Whether you'll be <u>living at home</u> while at university

Things to Know When Adding Your Choices

• If you <u>haven't decided</u> on all your courses yet, you <u>can still send</u> off your application with the <u>choices you've made</u> — you can then <u>add other courses</u> using <u>UCAS Track</u>.

• The <u>order</u> you put your choices in <u>doesn't indicate</u> which choice you <u>prefer</u>.

• The universities <u>can't see</u> where else you've <u>applied</u>.

Filling in Your Application

Enter Your Education Information

1) You'll be asked to list all the <u>schools, colleges and centres</u> that you attended throughout your <u>secondary education</u> (Years 7 to 13) and the <u>qualifications</u> you got at each one.

2) You also need to include any <u>qualifications</u> you're <u>currently studying</u> for (e.g. A-Levels and Extended Project). Put your <u>grade</u> for these as '<u>Pending</u>'.

3) If you're <u>re-sitting</u> an exam, <u>add</u> your <u>school</u> and the <u>grade</u> you got when you <u>first sat</u> the exam. Then you need to <u>enter</u> the <u>qualification</u> a second time and put the <u>result</u> as '<u>Pending</u>'.

4) You can also add <u>other qualifications</u> here, such as performing arts or music qualifications. These may be worth <u>UCAS points</u> (see page 16).

5) Filling out your education information can take a while, but it's <u>important</u> that you <u>take your time</u> and get everything <u>correct</u>. If you get <u>stuck</u>, ask your <u>school or college</u> for the <u>information</u> you need.

> Your referee will add your predicted grades to your application.

Add Any Employment Information

You can enter details about <u>jobs you've had</u> or <u>currently have</u> here. You'll need to give:

- Employer's <u>name</u> and <u>address</u>
- Job <u>description</u>
- <u>Start</u> and <u>end</u> date
- Whether you work(ed) <u>full-time</u> or <u>part-time</u>

Jerry had been told on multiple occasions to stop eating the merchandise.

Complete the Last Parts of the Application

You need to <u>enter</u> your <u>personal statement</u> — see pages 45-47 for more information.

→

You might need to add the <u>details</u> of the <u>person</u> writing your <u>reference</u>. <u>Speak</u> to your <u>school or college</u> about how to fill in this section, or if you're <u>applying independently</u> see page 79.

→

Finally, you'll have to <u>pay for</u> and <u>send</u> your <u>application</u>. If you're applying <u>through school or college</u>, they should let you know <u>how</u> the application will be <u>paid for</u>. If you're <u>applying independently</u>, enter your <u>payment details</u>.

I'm applying to study zoology — luckily I have excellent koalafications...

When you've finished filling out your application, you'll have the option to view all of your details on one page before submitting it. This is a good way to check for pesky errors and any information that may be missing.

Filling in Your Application

Rather than applying to university, my uncle set up *The College of Great Procrastination*. Here are some tips on how to put together an application for his college that will guarantee you a place there.

Find Inventive Ways to 'Complete' Your Application

You need to show your commitment to Procrastination Studies in the way you fill in your application. That way, you'll have plenty to talk about in your personal statement. Here are some things you could try:

- Download and print off the application form, then make an origami crane with every page.

- Print off the application form again. Make yourself a cup of tea or coffee and then spend some time thinking about unusual ways you could fill in your application, e.g. using invisible ink.

- Create a list of pseudonyms you could use, before deciding to be honest.

- Conduct very, very thorough research to make sure you're well suited to the course. I'd recommend painting your bedroom wall and then watching it dry — pure bliss.

- Before adding your employment information, doodle pictures related to as many different professions as you can. It will serve as a great portfolio in the interview.

Continue Showcasing Your Talent When You Eventually Apply

1) Submit your application as close to the deadline as possible — your chances of getting an offer could come down to how few seconds are left before the deadline.
2) After applying, ignore any correspondence you get from the college for at least a month.
3) Term starts in October, so start thinking about moving into your accommodation in November.

Testimonial from a Procrastination Studies Applicant

I was about to write this testimonial when I started wondering where the word 'testimonial' originated from. Naturally, I then spent the next few days researching other words and, before I knew it, I'd learnt Latin instead. — Hess E. Tait

Don't put off until tomorrow what you can do next week...

Finding innovative ways to procrastinate is the key to impressing my uncle — that's why he set up his college in the first place. Of course, it's just him in his living room at the moment, but I'm sure that'll change in the future...

The Personal Statement

Your personal statement is a chance to show universities that you're not just a set of grades or a UCAS ID number, but an intriguing, fascinating and devilishly charming individual that they'd be fools to pass up.

Your Personal Statement is Your Time to Shine

1) Your personal statement is a <u>piece of writing</u> that you submit as part of your <u>UCAS application</u>.

2) It needs to <u>explain why</u> you're <u>interested</u> in studying the subject you're applying for and to <u>show</u> admissions officers why you're a <u>desirable student</u>. You should include:

- why you're <u>excited</u> to study your chosen subject
- what you've done to <u>further your interest</u> in the subject — this can include interesting hobbies or clubs
- how your <u>skills</u> and <u>experience</u> make you stand out and make you the <u>ideal student</u> for the course
- what your <u>future goals</u> are and how the course will help you <u>achieve</u> them.

Hayami was pleased with how dazzling her personal statement was.

3) You need to do all of this in <u>4000 characters</u> or <u>47 lines</u> (whichever you reach first).

4) Your personal statement is <u>very important</u> — admissions officers look at <u>a large number</u> of different applications, so you want to make your statement really impressive and <u>memorable</u>.

You Only Get One Personal Statement

1) The <u>same personal statement</u> gets sent to <u>all</u> of your <u>choices</u>.

2) This means that while you need to tailor your personal statement to the <u>courses</u> you're applying for, you <u>shouldn't focus</u> on just <u>one choice</u> or you'll risk <u>alienating</u> the other universities.

3) This is particularly important if your <u>choices</u> have a lot of <u>differences</u>:

What to do if you're applying to courses with very different modules

- Look for any modules or topics that are covered in all of your choices and talk about these areas of the subject.
- Avoid naming a specific course or module — it may give away your preferred choice and put other universities off.

What to do if you're applying to courses for different subjects, e.g. maths and biology

- Make sure your statement is suitable for all of your subjects.
- Talk about your skills more generally and focus on ones that are relevant to both courses.

It's important to know that having a personal statement that talks about two very different subjects, e.g. sports science and zoology, can make it seem like you're not really committed to either. This could cost you an offer if it looks like you're not as passionate as other candidates.

The Personal Statement

Writing a Good Personal Statement Takes a Few Goes

Your personal statement is important, so you <u>shouldn't rush</u> it. It's also important not to panic if your <u>first attempt isn't perfect</u> — it'll take a <u>few drafts</u> to get it into peak university-stunning condition. Take a look at this <u>diagram</u> to see how to go about writing your statement:

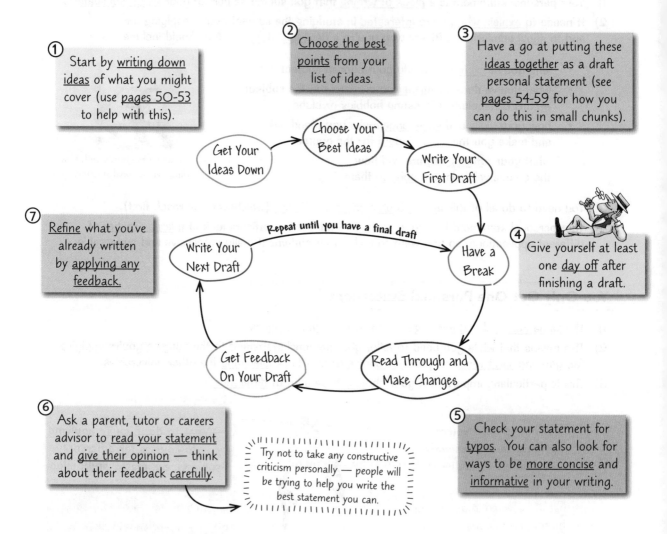

① Start by <u>writing down ideas</u> of what you might cover (use <u>pages 50-53</u> to help with this).

② <u>Choose the best points</u> from your list of ideas.

③ Have a go at putting these <u>ideas together</u> as a draft personal statement (see <u>pages 54-59</u> for how you can do this in small chunks).

⑦ <u>Refine</u> what you've already written by <u>applying any feedback.</u>

④ Give yourself at least one <u>day off</u> after finishing a draft.

⑥ Ask a parent, tutor or careers advisor to <u>read your statement</u> and <u>give their opinion</u> — think about their feedback <u>carefully</u>.

Try not to take any constructive criticism personally — people will be trying to help you write the best statement you can.

⑤ Check your statement for <u>typos</u>. You can also look for ways to be <u>more concise</u> and <u>informative</u> in your writing.

Get Your Ideas Down

Choose Your Best Ideas

Write Your First Draft

Repeat until you have a final draft

Write Your Next Draft

Have a Break

Get Feedback On Your Draft

Read Through and Make Changes

Eventually, you'll reach a point where you have a <u>polished</u> personal statement that's <u>ready to send</u>.

Don't write your personal statement straight into UCAS Apply

Write each <u>draft</u> of your personal statement in a <u>word processor</u>. When you've got your <u>final draft</u>, copy it over to <u>UCAS Apply</u> and <u>check</u> that nothing has gone wrong before you submit it.

The Personal Statement

You'll Need to Use Examples to Support Your Points

1) It's not enough to just <u>say what skills you have</u> in your personal statement — admissions officers will be expecting you to <u>provide examples</u> that <u>demonstrate the skills</u> you describe.

2) While it's good to talk about the <u>skills</u> you've gained from <u>school work</u>, it's likely that <u>other</u> students who are applying to the course <u>will also have these skills</u>.

3) To <u>distinguish yourself</u> from other applicants, you need to give examples of things that you've done <u>in your spare time</u>. Use these to demonstrate your <u>positive characteristics</u> and highlight what you're <u>passionate</u> about.

What your examples should include

✓ <u>Skills</u> that are <u>relevant</u> to your subject, e.g. essay writing for an English degree

✓ <u>Unique experiences</u> or <u>talents</u> that are linked to your subject, e.g. visiting interesting rock formations if you're applying for a Geology degree

✓ Skills or hobbies that show you can <u>contribute</u> to university life <u>outside of your course</u>, e.g. involvement with societies or sports teams

✓ A focus on <u>your achievements</u> rather than other people's — especially when talking about activities you've done as part of a <u>team</u>

Jake was proud of his double-denim look, but it did nothing to improve his communication skills.

What your examples should avoid

✗ Talking in detail about <u>skills</u> that <u>aren't relevant</u> to your course

✗ Talking about hobbies or experiences that <u>don't show</u> you <u>developing skills</u>, e.g. a beach holiday in the Caribbean

✗ Being too <u>vague</u> or <u>generic</u>, e.g. discussing work experience without really saying what you did

✗ <u>Exaggerating</u> or <u>lying</u> about your accomplishments

Don't Copy an Example Personal Statement

1) There are plenty of <u>example</u> personal statements in <u>books</u> and <u>online</u>. These can be <u>helpful</u> for <u>getting ideas</u> of what to say in your statement.

2) However, you <u>mustn't copy</u> these or any other statements. UCAS has a system to <u>detect plagiarism</u> and if you're caught, the <u>universities</u> you've applied to will be <u>informed</u> — this can <u>jeopardise your application</u>.

Nina's system of finding plagiarised statements involved using her psychic powers.

I've written plenty of statements before — but this time, it's personal...

Writing a personal statement is a bit of a mammoth task, but breaking it up into a number of smaller jobs can make it easier. Start by getting your ideas together and then shape those into sentences and paragraphs later.

How to Stand Out From the Crowd

There are lots of extra-curricular activities that can show off your skills and passion for a subject. Take a look at how these people stand out from the crowd. Psst — their biggest secret is not being in greyscale...

Write About Your Hobbies

1) Creative hobbies, such as making art, producing videos or writing for a blog, show that you have creative talent and are self-motivated — this is particularly useful for degrees where you'd spend a lot of time studying independently.

2) Playing a sport or being part of a club shows that you have interests outside of your studies. It also helps to demonstrate skills like leadership (e.g. if you're a captain or chairperson), teamwork (if you do things as part of a squad or group) and dedication to something.

You can also mention any competitions you've participated in, e.g. dance, athletics or business competitions, especially if you won or placed highly. This will emphasise your talent and show that you're able to organise yourself and meet deadlines.

Discuss Any Work Experience

1) Writing about work or volunteering experience can be a good way to show that you have transferable skills, such as communication skills and the ability to work with others, which are important for university life.

2) Try to get work experience or an internship somewhere that is relevant to your course, e.g. in a veterinary practice if you want to study veterinary medicine. This will show that you're committed to your subject and may already have subject-specific knowledge.

3) Volunteering is a good way of showing that you have a strong work-ethic and selfless characteristics. Many places are on the lookout for volunteers, such as charity shops, local festivals and libraries.

4) You can also write about any voluntary activities you've done at school, such as peer mentoring, sitting on the school council or organising school events. If you've given back to your school like this, it suggests to universities that you can contribute to university life.

Chris learnt more about staring into cameras during his work experience than he did about construction.

How to Stand Out From the Crowd

Refer to Extra Courses and Summer Schools

1) Completing <u>courses</u>, such as free massive open online courses (MOOCs), can increase your <u>level of knowledge</u> and sometimes lead to you gaining a <u>qualification</u>. Doing these in your own time shows that you have a really strong <u>interest in your subject</u> and a desire to <u>continue your studies independently</u>.

2) Taking part in <u>awards programmes</u> like the Duke of Edinburgh's Award shows that you're willing to take on <u>new challenges</u> and can reach an <u>impressive standard</u> of <u>achievement</u>.

3) Doing an <u>EPQ</u> (Extended Project Qualification) is a good way to show that you have important <u>independent study skills</u>.

4) Attending a <u>summer school</u> is a great way to show that you can <u>adapt</u> to new working and living environments, which is a <u>big part</u> of <u>attending university</u>.

If you want to <u>study abroad</u> as part of your course, consider applying to a summer school in a <u>different country</u>. This can show your ability to work with people from <u>different cultures</u> and prove that you're capable of <u>living and working abroad</u>.

Mention Wider Reading or Listening

1) Taking the time to <u>read</u> and <u>listen</u> to extra material that's <u>related to your subject</u> can be a good way of <u>increasing your knowledge</u> and showing your <u>continued interest</u>.

2) You can read or listen to a <u>range of things</u>, such as academic journals, articles, books, lectures, podcasts, blogs and videos. Engaging with a wide range of materials emphasises the <u>depth of your interest</u>.

3) Try to stay <u>up-to-date</u> with the <u>latest news</u> and <u>developments</u> related to your subject by reading newspapers and looking online — it shows that you have an understanding of the <u>latest trends</u>.

The activities on these pages aren't the only ones you could talk about, and the skills mentioned aren't the only ones you can gain from them. You'll need to think about your experience and what will be most relevant to your application.

I wanted to stand out from the crowd — that's why I moved to the countryside...

If you haven't done any extra-curricular activities then you should start now. Depending on when you're reading this, it might be too late to do some things, but you can always do some wider reading or find a new hobby.

Writing a Personal Statement

Getting Your Thoughts Down

It can be really tricky to know where to start when writing your personal statement. Fear not — these next few pages aim to help you come up with some ideas and get your creative juices flowing. Mmm, juice...

Think About Why You're Interested in the Subject

1) Think about what first <u>sparked your interest</u> — things that are unusual or unique can help you <u>stand out</u>.

2) You could also consider whether your <u>school subjects</u> or any <u>specific modules</u> fuelled your interest.

3) Remember that university tutors and lecturers are <u>experts</u> in their subject — they want to make sure they're working with people who are just as <u>enthusiastic</u>.

Look at the <u>mind map</u> on the right about Lauren's interest in Food Art Studies, then <u>fill in</u> the space below with the reasons why <u>you're interested</u> in <u>your chosen subject</u>.

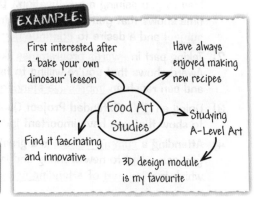

EXAMPLE:

First interested after a 'bake your own dinosaur' lesson

Have always enjoyed making new recipes

Food Art Studies

Find it fascinating and innovative

Studying A-Level Art

3D design module is my favourite

Use these white spaces in whatever way works best for you — you don't necessarily have to draw a mind map.

Lauren's apple desserts were frighteningly delicious.

You don't have to fill in these pages in one go — you can come back and add more things as you think of them.

Writing a Personal Statement

Getting Your Thoughts Down

Consider How You've Followed Up Your Interest

1) Jot down any <u>extra-curricular activities</u> you've done that are related to your chosen subject. See <u>pages 48-49</u> for the types of things you could write down.

2) Make a brief note about the <u>impact</u> your activity has had, either on <u>yourself</u> or on <u>those around you</u>.

> Look at the <u>example</u> on the right about how Lauren has followed up her interest in Food Art Studies, then <u>fill in</u> the space below with the ways you've <u>followed up</u> your interest in <u>your chosen subject</u>.

EXAMPLE:

Founded my school's Food Art Club
- Built a community of food art fans
- Learnt new techniques from other students

Runner-up in regional baking contest
- Highly commended for original ideas
- Learnt to produce food under time pressure

Lauren made an artistic cake for her birthday-forgetting partner.

The greatest food artist is either Leonardo da Minty or Vincent van Dough...

You don't have to have cured all disease or created an artistic masterpiece to show your passion for a subject (although you should definitely mention it if you have) — simpler efforts discussed well can be just as effective.

Getting Your Thoughts Down

Think About What Skills Make You A Good Candidate

1) Universities will want to see that you have the skills to <u>succeed</u> on their <u>course</u>.

2) Think about any relevant <u>skills</u> you have and then think of <u>evidence</u> that demonstrates them.

3) It might be helpful to look at the <u>courses</u> you're applying to and look for any <u>common skills</u> that are needed. Think of <u>things you've done</u> that show you have these skills.

Look at the <u>example</u> on the right about the skills Lauren has that prepare her for Food Art Studies, then <u>fill in</u> the space below with your own <u>skills</u> and <u>evidence</u>.

Skill / Strength	Evidence
Experienced Cook	• Passed an advanced cooking course • Taken part in regional cooking competitions
Scientific Knowledge	• Studying A-Level Chemistry & Biology — they include modules about proteins and enzymes
Creativity	• Run a food blog — this also improves my writing and organisational skills • Studying A-Level Art — I have experience with different mediums, e.g. paint, clay, ceramics, etc.
Confident Sharing Ideas	• Often share subjective ideas in Art classes • Give feedback on dishes at Food Art Club

Lauren enjoyed making the owl the most — it was a hoot.

Getting Your Thoughts Down

Consider How The Course Will Help Your Future Goals

1) Explaining your <u>motivation</u> for choosing a course will reassure universities that you're <u>unlikely</u> to <u>drop out</u>.

2) You might apply for a course so you can go onto <u>further study</u>, or because it'll help you get your <u>dream job</u>.

3) Think about the <u>specific skills</u> and <u>qualifications</u> you'll gain from the course and how these <u>link</u> to your goals.

Look at the <u>mind map</u> on the right about how Food Art Studies will help Lauren achieve her <u>future goals</u>, then <u>fill in</u> the space below with how <u>your chosen course</u> will help you <u>achieve yours</u>.

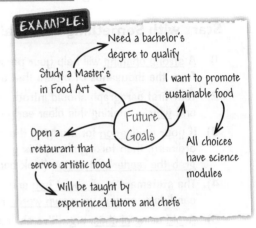

EXAMPLE:

Need a bachelor's degree to qualify

Study a Master's in Food Art

I want to promote sustainable food

Future Goals

Open a restaurant that serves artistic food

All choices have science modules

Will be taught by experienced tutors and chefs

Don't worry if you don't know what career you want yet. You can still think about short-term goals that show your interest in (and your ambition to study) your chosen course.

Lauren's next goal was to eat all the cakes.

I'm now craving a top personal statement and cake — lots and lots of cake...

After you've jotted some notes down, look back on everything you've come up with and then turn the page for some cake. And by cake, I mean something just as delicious — pages that will help you to develop your notes...

Developing Your Ideas

Now you've got some thoughts down, it's time to start fleshing them out and thinking about how you might structure them. These pages show one way you might organise your ideas, but it's not the only way.

Start with Something Personal

1) A <u>strong opening</u> will help your personal statement <u>stand out</u> from the thousands of others that admissions tutors will read.

2) Your first paragraph should introduce <u>what you want to study</u> and <u>why</u> — making this clear early on will help a lot.

3) If your <u>motivation</u> for studying the subject is a bit out of the ordinary, then talking about this <u>unusual or unique reason</u> can <u>grab the reader's attention</u> (look back at your notes on p.50).

4) The statement is <u>all about you</u> and why you are a really great candidate, so <u>use your own words</u> rather than quoting someone else.

5) <u>Avoid</u> using <u>clichés</u>, e.g. "I've always loved dentistry..."

Gemma was convinced that she had everything she needed to start her personal statement.

Look at these <u>example openings</u> to some personal statements, then <u>write</u> a couple of sentences to <u>start</u> your own <u>when you're ready</u>.

> Some people find it easier to write the start of their personal statement later on, once they know what they're going to write about.

ARCHAEOLOGY

My first introduction to archaeology was the discovery of a ruined Roman villa in my town. This started an interest that I have developed ever since, and which has motivated my decision to study the subject at university.

MUSIC

I am constantly amazed by the power that music has to communicate emotion across cultural and linguistic barriers. This is something I first experienced while performing at an international festival with my choir, and it is partly why I am so eager to continue my musical studies at university.

Developing Your Ideas

Explain Why You're Interested in the Subject

1) One of the biggest challenges when writing a personal statement is <u>showing that you're passionate</u> about the subject without actually saying "I'm passionate" — it's a big cliché.

2) Look back at the notes you made about your interest on p.50. Elaborating on these ideas in your personal statement will offer <u>proof of your enthusiasm</u> for the subject.

3) <u>Don't make up reasons</u> for your interest in the subject because you think they sound impressive. Include <u>genuine reasons</u> about <u>why you love it</u> and <u>why you want to study it</u> at university.

> Look at these <u>examples</u> of people writing about their <u>interest</u>, then <u>write</u> a couple of sentences about your interest below.

ITALIAN

My A-Level in Italian has increased my love for the language and culture. I have particularly enjoyed the theme focusing on the evolution of Italian society. It has been fascinating to learn about the impact of migration and the cultural differences that are found in various regions of the country.

EDUCATION STUDIES

I am particularly interested in the use of technology in the classroom, especially with the recent rise of virtual reality software. Its potential to engage pupils and promote curiosity across a range of subjects fascinates me. For example, students could study human anatomy by exploring organs and tissues in virtual space.

_____

_____

_____

_____

Some students have a vested interest in wanting to study fashion...

When you're writing your personal statement, it's really important to make sure that you explain the examples you discuss — this helps admissions tutors to understand your interest in the subject and your thoughts on it.

Developing Your Ideas

Show How You've Developed Your Interest

1) You can use your <u>passion</u> for the subject as a <u>springboard</u> to talk about <u>how you've followed up</u> that interest.

2) Flick back to the activities you jotted down on p.51 — writing about these in your personal statement shows that you've been <u>motivated to learn more</u> about your chosen subject <u>in your own time</u>.

3) Make it clear that you've <u>reflected</u> on the activities and have <u>learnt or gained</u> something from them. It's much better to focus on <u>one or two examples</u> in depth than it is to reel off a list — it shows that you've <u>engaged properly</u> with what you were doing.

Max was hopeful that his innovative use of French literature would impress admissions tutors.

Look at these <u>examples</u> of how people have <u>developed their interest</u>, then <u>write</u> a couple of sentences about how you've developed yours.

CRIMINOLOGY

Eager to develop my interest in criminology, I took a FutureLearn course on Forensic Psychology. This gave me a compelling insight into how eyewitness evidence is used, and also abused, in the criminal justice system. I would love to build on this understanding by studying criminology at a higher level.

DET. COOK

HISTORY

After reading a book about Ignatius Sancho, a vocal opponent of the slave trade, I started thinking more deeply about black history in the UK. This led me to visit the Black Cultural Archives in London, which enhanced my understanding of this less widely known history, and I hope to explore this area more through further study.

Developing Your Ideas

Expand on Your Skills and Strengths

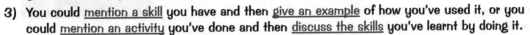

1) Discussing your most <u>relevant skills</u> from p.52 will demonstrate your <u>ability</u> to <u>study at university</u>.

2) You might want to <u>prioritise</u> skills that are mentioned in <u>entry requirements</u> or <u>course details</u>, but you can also talk about skills that will prepare you for university life in general, such as organisational skills.

3) You could <u>mention a skill</u> you have and then <u>give an example</u> of how you've used it, or you could <u>mention an activity</u> you've done and then <u>discuss the skills</u> you've learnt by doing it.

4) <u>Linking examples</u> back to the <u>course</u> is a good way of showing you're aware of what skills you need.

> Look at these <u>examples</u> of people writing about <u>their skills</u>, then <u>write</u> a couple of sentences about a skill of your own.

POLITICS

At college, I chair the debate club, which meets every Wednesday. This has enabled me to work on my leadership and communication skills, as well as my ability to carefully consider both sides of an argument. A politics degree would allow me to develop these skills in a more formal context.

MATHS

I'm excited to study a degree in mathematics as it will allow me to continue improving my problem-solving skills. By working part-time in a call centre, I already have experience using these skills to find solutions to customer problems. This is something I find really rewarding.

I have all the right skills for a degree in architecture — I'm a pillar of strengths...

Some skills, like independence and time management, will be useful for every degree, while others are more specific to certain subjects. Make sure that you include strengths that are relevant to your chosen subject.

Developing Your Ideas

Explain How the Subject Will Help Your Future Goals

1) Writing about how further study will <u>help you achieve your goals</u> shows the admissions tutors that <u>you have ambition</u>.

2) Flick back to the notes you made on p.53. Instead of <u>writing a full section</u> about these goals, you could talk about them in <u>other parts</u> of your <u>statement</u>.

3) For example, you could include them <u>after</u> mentioning some <u>work experience</u>, or use them as a way to <u>bring your statement to a close</u>.

Radzi fell to his knees when he realised how wide of the mark he'd been talking about his goals.

Look at these <u>examples</u> of people discussing their <u>future aspirations</u>, then <u>write</u> a couple of sentences about how your chosen subject links to <u>your own goals</u>.

ACCOUNTING

This work experience confirmed that accounting is the right profession for me, and I strongly believe that the skills and experience gained from an accounting degree would help me along the path to becoming a chartered accountant.

MEDICINAL CHEMISTRY

I am fascinated by medicinal chemistry and would love the chance to explore this area of the subject more during my studies. The opportunity to carry out research in this area is exciting and would support my aspirations of finding work in this field after university.

Developing Your Ideas

End with a Reminder of Why You're Right For the Course

1) The ending of your personal statement should be a <u>quick summary</u> of the <u>key reasons</u> why you should be offered a place — just make sure you're <u>not repeating</u> what you said earlier.

2) It should be concise, so try to get your point across in <u>no more than a few sentences</u>.

3) <u>Avoid using a quote</u> — the university wants to remember what you've said, not somebody else.

4) It can be a good place to talk about your <u>goals</u> — this leaves the impression that you're <u>looking to the future</u> when thinking about your chosen subject.

Look at these <u>example endings</u>, then <u>write</u> a couple of sentences for <u>your own ending</u>.

GEOGRAPHY

Recent environmental issues have confirmed to me that geography is as important and relevant as ever. I feel that university would be the perfect place to further my understanding of the subject and build on the skills I have already gained, alongside people who share my passion for the world we live in .

Anada took the advice to sum everything up a bit too literally.

MEDICINE

After my experience shadowing doctors on a palliative care ward and volunteering at a local care home, I know beyond a doubt that medicine is the path for me. I believe that my commitment, scientific knowledge and empathy will help me to overcome the challenges that a career in medicine presents and allow me to make a positive impact in the world.

All good things must come to an end — even this page...

I know, I'm sad about it too. Luckily for you though, we've still got four whole pages to go before we're done with this section. Just like the magic porridge pot, personal statements are the gift that keeps on giving — nom.

Example Personal Statements

Next up we have two example personal statements — I know, I know, it's just what you've always wanted.

Here's an Example of a Good Personal Statement

Read this example of an English Literature personal statement and then look at the annotations to see what it does well.

This statement would be 47 lines and 3864 characters long in the UCAS form.

Interesting opening that makes it clear what they are applying for.

Ends their introduction by emphasising their passion for the subject.

From Shakespeare to science fiction, postcolonial literature to graphic novels, I have always enjoyed reading a wide range of texts. My love of English Literature stems from its ability to make me rethink my own preconceptions, but studying it at A-Level has given me greater scope to explore the ways in which different genres can inspire readers to consider the world more carefully. I am excited about furthering this exploration at university.

Shows their engagement with subject and what they find interesting about it.

Expands on this example with more detail about why it interests them.

This curiosity led me to write a comparison of John Keats's poem 'To Autumn' and Aldous Huxley's novel 'Brave New World' for my Extended Project. While Romanticism and dystopian fiction might seem wildly different at first glance, thinking about the texts in depth convinced me of their similarities. Both explore relationships that are particularly relevant in light of today's challenges; the relationship between humans and nature in Keats's poem, and the relationship between humans and technology in 'Brave New World'. Both also have an enduring resonance which I think demonstrates literature's power to challenge readers' perceptions of the world around them.

Introduces a specific example to illustrate their interest.

Incorporates other studies when relevant.

Talks about something unusual, which makes them stand out.

After studying the effects of climate change as part of my Biology A-Level, I decided to read more about it in my own time and discovered the emerging climate fiction genre. Literature that addresses this environmental crisis is not widely studied and has not achieved the popularity of other genres, but it surprised me to learn that the foundations for climate fiction were laid in the 1960s, with works such as J.G. Ballard's 'The Drowned World'. This novel imagines a world where solar activity has led to rising temperatures and flooding and the world has devolved to a state that resembles the Triassic period. The protagonists, however, are drawn to the destruction, and observe their new habitat with a compulsion that

Introduces how they've developed their interest in the subject outside school.

Gives a specific example of how they've followed this interest up further.

Example Personal Statements

Gives a detailed explanation of what they've learnt from this further reading

allows the reader to witness the full extent of the catastrophe. I was struck by this stark depiction of human nature in response to climate change. Their reactions in the face of approaching destruction reflect current events with an eerie accuracy, and I was impressed with the way it made me reconsider my own behaviour. I am intrigued by the potential for climate fiction to enact real-world change by challenging people's perceptions in this way.

My desire to explore new areas of literature and how it can influence people is something I have followed up through my participation in a local reading group. The group meets weekly and I have taken on an increasing level of responsibility. I help to organise discussion groups, author talks and presentations on books. This has honed my presenting skills, as well as my commitment and organisational skills, which will be vital at university. I recently took on the role of stage manager during a run of 'Death of a Salesman' at my local amateur dramatics group. This not only gave me a greater understanding of plays in general, but also allowed me to approach literature from a new angle and think about how the written word can affect people differently when performed. I also work part-time as a retail assistant. Besides requiring strong time management skills, this job has also helped me to develop my communication and problem-solving skills, as I interact with customers and handle their complaints.

Talks about a relevant extra-curricular activity which makes them stand out from the crowd.

They highlight the skills they've gained from the activity and link it back to the course.

Links a recreational activity back to the course in a relevant way and shows they have more to offer the university.

I hope to continue developing these skills through further study, and eventually use them to teach English in secondary schools after my degree. This would allow me to share my love of literature and see how it continues to evolve and challenge readers in new and exciting ways. I believe that my combination of skills and experience has more than prepared me to study English Literature at a higher level, and I am confident that I will be able to work independently, balance my commitments and engage fully with the course.

Expands on their skills by considering how the course will help with their future plans.

Ends with a clear, concise summary of their key points.

It's important to remember that this is just one example...

You don't necessarily need this much textual analysis in your personal statement — everyone's statement is different and should focus on the skills you'll need for your subject. The most important thing is to play to your strengths.

Example Personal Statements

It's also handy to think about what makes a 'not-so-good' statement so you can avoid falling into those traps.

Here's an Example of a Personal Statement That Needs More Work

Read this example of a Physics personal statement and then look at the annotations. It's written by a really passionate student who has the ability to stand out from the crowd, but they don't communicate their skills and abilities in the right way.

This statement would be 46 lines and 3419 characters long in the UCAS form.

Starts with a quote rather than their own words.

Uses clichés.

Their first mention of physics in an academic context is too brief.

They don't sound confident in their own abilities — you don't want to be arrogant, but try to sound assured.

Fails to explain what skills have been gained from the activities.

As the great physicist Lise Meitner once wrote, "I love physics with all my heart. I can hardly imagine it not being a part of my life." These are words which I echo. I have loved physics since I was a child. I remember watching 'The Sky at Night' with my grandparents and being amazed at everything I could learn about the universe. I have a thirst for knowledge, and physics taught me to look beyond the boundaries of my own imagination and dream of the impossible.

At college, I am studying A-Levels in Physics, Maths, Further Maths and Music, and I am achieving highly in all of them. My favourite module in the A-Level Physics course is Astrophysics, and this interest comes from the Nobel Prize-winning work on gravitational waves.

I think that I'm a very talented and determined student and I probably have what it takes to succeed at university. Throughout my time at primary school, I played football with my local team. This taught me teamwork skills and I realised that I am very sporty. I am now a long-distance runner (I have successfully completed two half-marathons) and the captain of my college's hockey team. In addition to sports, I am passionate about music. I enjoy studying Music at A-Level, have played the saxophone since I was seven and currently play in a jazz band. We have rehearsals once a week and our concerts are very popular. I also work at a computer repair shop on Saturdays, which means I have good technical and time management skills.

They never mention wanting to study physics in their introduction.

They don't give enough detail to explain their interest.

Uses a really old example of a skill rather than something more relevant.

There's no mention of why these skills will help them succeed on the course.

Example Personal Statements

Makes it sound like physics is less important than other activities.

The rest of my spare time is devoted to physics. I constantly read about the subject to expand my knowledge of it beyond what is taught on the A-Level syllabus. My favourite books include 'Cosmos' by Carl Sagan, 'The Feynman Lectures on Physics' by Richard P. Feynman, and 'Relativity: The Special and the General Theory' by Albert Einstein. I also found Steven Hawking's 'A Brief History of Time' very interesting. This extra reading has ensured that I have a detailed understanding of physics at a more advanced level than what I have been taught in school. I also write a blog about physics, which I update once a fortnight with an article about the latest developments in physics and science more generally. I enjoy keeping this blog as it motivates me to stay up-to-date with the latest physics news, and I am continually learning more about my subject.

Doesn't offer specific examples of how this further reading has improved their understanding.

Repeats what they said at the start of the paragraph.

Spells 'Stephen' incorrectly — hasn't checked the statement for typos or mistakes.

Writing style often lacks variety — most sentences start with 'I'.

I also volunteer as a Student Ambassador in the physics department at my college. We visit local primary schools on Wednesday afternoons and run physics workshops with the children. We show them basic experiments to try to interest them in the subject from a young age and introduce them to some of the main ideas that physics is about. I am happy to have the opportunity to spread my enthusiasm for physics to younger students who might follow in my footsteps in the future.

Mentions a good activity but needs to focus more on what's been gained and how it prepares them for the course.

I have not really decided what I would like to do for a career. I might do a PhD, or get a job, or focus on my music.

Future goals are vague and unrelated to the course.

Clichéd ending.

Conclusion repeats earlier points without adding anything new.

In conclusion, physics is my favourite subject and something that I am incredibly passionate about. I cannot imagine studying any other subject at university. I am independent, dedicated, organised and talented, as shown by my combination of A-Levels but also by the various activities that I take part in, including jazz band, the hockey team and my part-time job. I am an excellent student who is excited to study physics at university in Leeds.

The focus on studying physics at university only comes at the end, and they also mention a specific place.

Avoid writing jokes in your personal statement — jokes are the worst...

And with that, we've reached the end of this whopper of a section. Put the kettle on, take a break, then have a go at writing your first draft. Keep looking back at the notes you've made in this book to help focus your writing.

Interviews

Depending on which universities and courses you apply to, you might be asked to attend an interview. The next few pages will talk you through what to expect if you're invited to one and how you can prepare.

Interviews Help Universities Get to Know You

1) Along with your written application, some universities use interviews to <u>get an idea</u> of how you <u>think and work</u>. This helps them to decide whether you're a <u>good fit</u> for the <u>course</u> you've applied to.

2) Interviews aren't only important for the university to <u>get to know you</u> though — they're also an <u>opportunity</u> for you to find out more about the <u>university</u> and the <u>course</u>.

Edward prepared for his interview by getting to know himself.

Interviews Can Involve Different Tasks

The <u>style</u> of your interview might differ depending on the <u>university</u> and <u>course</u>. Here are some of the <u>most common</u> things you might be <u>asked to do</u>:

You might also have to do additional tests (see pages 68-69).

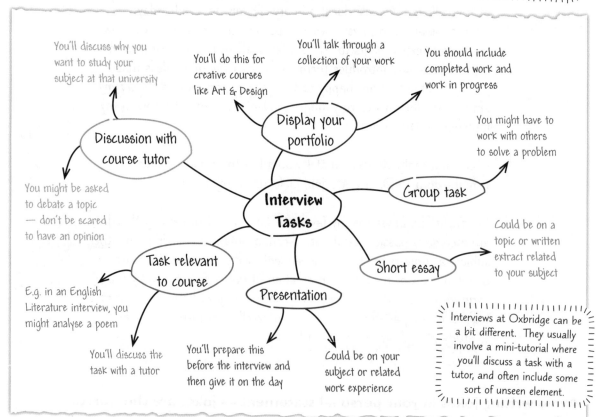

You'll discuss why you want to study your subject at that university

You'll do this for creative courses like Art & Design

You'll talk through a collection of your work

You should include completed work and work in progress

Discussion with course tutor

Display your portfolio

You might have to work with others to solve a problem

You might be asked to debate a topic — don't be scared to have an opinion

Interview Tasks

Group task

Could be on a topic or written extract related to your subject

Task relevant to course

Short essay

E.g. in an English Literature interview, you might analyse a poem

Presentation

You'll discuss the task with a tutor

You'll prepare this before the interview and then give it on the day

Could be on your subject or related work experience

Interviews at Oxbridge can be a bit different. They usually involve a mini-tutorial where you'll discuss a task with a tutor, and often include some sort of unseen element.

Interviews

Tutors Look For Certain Characteristics

Tutors won't expect you to be an expert, but they will want to see that you have these qualities:

- Willingness to engage with new ideas and to tackle unexpected problems — interviewers are just as interested in how you make your decision or reach an answer as they are in what you do or the answer you give.

- Confidence to correct own ~~misstakes~~ mistakes.

- Honesty — it's okay not to know the answer or to ask for further explanation.

- Enthusiasm for the subject — talk about topics you're interested in.

- A positive attitude — avoid speaking badly about people you've worked with.

Not All Universities Will Have Interviews

1) Certain universities and courses are more likely to interview because there's more competition for places.

2) If you apply to Oxford or Cambridge, pass any additional tests and they're interested in you, they'll ask you to an interview before considering whether to offer you a place.

3) Other universities and courses might also have interviews — check the course description to see if you'll have to do an interview.

4) If you're applying for a joint honours course, you'll likely be interviewed by tutors from both subjects.

The Usual Suspects
Universities
Oxford   Cambridge
Imperial College London   University College London
Courses
Medicine   Dentistry   Nursing
Art & Design   Education   Performing Arts

Universities Will Contact You For Interviews

1) If you're invited to an interview, you'll either be contacted directly by the university, or you'll find out on UCAS Track.

2) You'll likely be given some extra information about what will happen on the day (see p.64). However, if you feel you need more information, contact the university.

3) If you can't attend the interview on the specified date, tell the university as soon as possible so that they can make other arrangements.

Jim was pleasantly surprised when the university contacted him by carrier pigeon.

The tutor interviewing me asked if I was okay — I said, "No, I'm Susan..."

There's a lot to process when you're in an interview, and at times you might not understand what's being asked of you. Don't be scared to ask for clarification if you need it — you'll be able to give a much better answer afterwards.

How to Prepare for an Interview

Whether it's your first interview or your fifth, there are plenty of things you can do to prepare. The next few pages will give you an idea of how to make the process run as smoothly as a hamster on a well-oiled wheel.

Plan How You'll Get There

1) Find out <u>where</u> you need to go and for <u>what time</u>. See if the <u>university has a map</u> on their website to help you find the <u>right building</u>.

2) Work out <u>how you'll get there</u> — car, train, hot air balloon, etc. Have a <u>back-up journey plan</u> in case of <u>delays</u> or <u>cancellations</u>.

3) Plan to arrive with <u>plenty of time before</u> your interview.

4) Some universities offer <u>overnight accommodation</u> for the night before your interview, so it's a good idea to <u>check if this is available</u>.

Daniela hoped that her back-up transport would get her to the interview on time.

Look Over Your Research of the University and Course

1) <u>Refresh</u> your <u>knowledge</u> of the <u>university</u> and <u>course</u>, especially <u>specific information</u> like what each <u>module offers</u> and details about the <u>university's facilities</u>.

2) Write a <u>list</u> of things that you'd like to get <u>more information</u> about at the interview. For example:

- How your <u>contact hours</u> will be divided between <u>lectures</u> and <u>seminars</u>.
- The <u>assessment methods</u> used on the course (e.g. presentations, group work, essays).
- More detail about the <u>academic</u> and <u>personal support</u> that's available.

> Try not to ask questions that you can find the answer to easily, e.g. the types of modules offered on the course. This might make it look like you haven't done your research.

Get Ready to Answer Questions

1) Use your <u>research</u> about the university to get a clear idea of <u>why you want to study there</u>.

2) <u>Re-read</u> your <u>application</u> (especially your <u>personal statement</u>) and think about what the university could <u>ask</u> you about, e.g. A-Level topics, background reading, work experience, etc.

3) Read the news and stay <u>updated</u> with the latest <u>developments</u> in your chosen subject.

4) Think about your <u>strengths</u> and <u>weaknesses</u> and <u>what you do</u> to try and <u>improve</u> yourself.

Some Common Interview Questions

- Why did you apply to this university?
- Why do you want to study this subject?
- Why is this subject relevant today?
- What are you best at?
- What is something you find difficult?

How to Prepare for an Interview

Practise Answering Questions

1) Try having a mock interview with a family member, teacher or member of a local Rotary Club.

2) Answering questions out loud to yourself will also help you feel more comfortable talking about things.

3) Practise keeping your answers concise — start with a simple point, give a relevant example and then build on this with a short explanation. Look at these example answers to a question about why a student wants to study Primary Education at a particular university:

GOOD EXAMPLE

Starts with a specific reason and shows knowledge of the course.

This Primary Education course appeals to me because of the module about children who learn English as an additional language. Volunteering to read with children at my local primary school taught me ways to help improve their reading ability, but I'm eager to learn new strategies so I can help even more children get comfortable with the English language.

Gives an example of where interest came from.

Says what they'll gain from the course and why it's important.

NOT-SO-GOOD EXAMPLE

Gives quite a general point.

Example doesn't link very well to the course.

I would like to do a degree in Primary Education because I'm really interested in working with children. Growing up, I did lots of babysitting and I'd like to learn more about how children develop.

Explanation is vague and doesn't convey enthusiasm.

Make Your Final Preparations

1) Decide what you're going to wear before the day of the interview. Check with the university what they'd like you to wear — it'll either be smart (e.g. a suit or dress) or smart-casual (e.g. smart trousers and a jumper).

2) Make a note of the university's contact details so you can let them know if you're going to be late.

3) Set an alarm the night before your interview so that you wake up with plenty of time to get everything ready.

4) Try to get a good night's sleep and eat a healthy breakfast before the interview.

5) If you're taking public transport, check it is running on time.

Things to Take to an Interview

- [x] Water and a snack
- [x] Your portfolio and any other documents you need
- [x] A notepad and multiple pens
- [x] Your phone (but switch it off during your interview)
- [x] A map or timetable if available

Because I wear camouflage, I always get asked to come interview...

After an interview, write down the questions you were asked, good answers you gave and anything you learned that could come in handy. Every interview you have will give you experience that will help in future interviews.

Additional Tests

It turns out your academic exams might not be the only tests you need to do. Yay... Don't worry though, these pages will give you an idea of why you could be asked to take a test and what sort of test it could be.

You Might Need to do Additional Tests

1) <u>Some courses</u> require that you take an <u>additional test</u> either before or during your interview.

2) These tests <u>assess</u> your <u>knowledge</u> about the <u>subject</u> and / or <u>related skills</u>.

3) You should check the <u>course descriptions</u> for your choices to see whether you need to sit any tests and <u>how to register</u> for them if you do.

4) You'll need to find out <u>when</u> you're allowed to <u>take each test</u>. Some have to be taken <u>the year before</u> the <u>course starts</u> and some can only be taken <u>once per year</u>.

5) You'll also need to know <u>where</u> to take any tests — they can usually <u>only be taken</u> at <u>test centres</u>.

Most Conservatoire Courses Require an Audition

If you're applying to a <u>conservatoire</u>, you'll likely have to do an audition <u>after</u> the <u>application deadline</u>.

1. The audition normally involves a <u>performance element</u> along with a <u>traditional interview</u>.

2. You'll <u>audition</u> at the <u>institutions you've applied</u> to, although some conservatoires hold auditions in <u>other locations</u>. If you're a <u>non-UK applicant</u>, you might be able to audition in <u>your country</u> or submit an <u>online audition</u>.

3. The conservatoire will let you know what <u>to prepare for your audition</u>, but if you have any questions, <u>get in touch</u> with them.

For more about applying to conservatoires, see page 27.

The LNAT is Used For Some Law Courses

1) The LNAT (Law National Aptitude Test) examines whether you have the <u>skills to study law</u>, e.g. <u>reasoning</u> and <u>analysing information</u>. It's more focused on this than your knowledge of law as a subject.

2) The test lasts <u>2 hours and 15 minutes</u> and is made up of <u>two sections</u>:

- The first section is a set of <u>multiple-choice questions</u> based on some <u>texts</u>.
- The second section is an <u>essay-style question</u>.

3) Make sure to check <u>which test session</u> your university wants you to sit <u>before you register</u>.

Isabelle was sure her talent for counting would help with any additional tests.

Additional Tests

There Are Specific Tests For Medical and Dental Applicants

If you're applying for medicine, dentistry, or other medical courses like biomedicine, you might have to take the UCAT (University Clinical Aptitude Test), BMAT (BioMedical Admissions Test) or both.

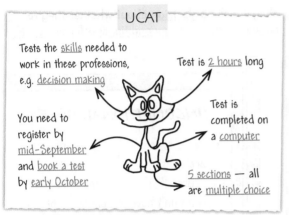

UCAT

Tests the skills needed to work in these professions, e.g. decision making

Test is 2 hours long

Test is completed on a computer

You need to register by mid-September and book a test by early October

5 sections — all are multiple choice

If you sit your test(s) in September, you might even be able to find out your result before you apply to UCAS.

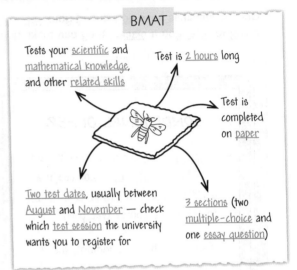

BMAT

Tests your scientific and mathematical knowledge, and other related skills

Test is 2 hours long

Test is completed on paper

Two test dates, usually between August and November — check which test session the university wants you to register for

3 sections (two multiple-choice and one essay question)

Oxbridge Ask Most Applicants to Complete Additional Tests

1) Oxford and Cambridge may get you to do at least one additional test. You can see which tests you need to complete on the entry requirements for your course. Some examples include:

ELAT (English Literature Admissions Test)

- For English courses
- Tests close reading skills and ability to construct a response
- Comparative essay on two unseen texts

TSA (Thinking Skills Assessment)

- For some subjects including Psychology and Economics
- Tests problem solving and critical thinking
- Multiple-choice questions and a writing task

PAT (Physics Aptitude Test)

- For Physics, Engineering, and Materials Science
- Tests A-Level Maths and Physics knowledge
- Multiple choice and other question types

2) Cambridge also requires you to complete a Supplementary Application Questionnaire (SAQ) via email. This gives them additional information that you haven't included on your UCAS application, such as topics you've covered at A-Level and your class sizes.

I've been told I should register for the UCAT — but I think I need HELP...

While tests can be scary, there are lots of resources available to help you prepare. Learn as much as you can about any tests that you're required to do by researching them and doing timed practice papers where possible.

Offers

So, you've done all the work, you've sent off your application and now you're waiting to get a response. Have a read of what universities might have to offer you — unfortunately, it's unlikely to be a free holiday...

There Are Different Types of Offers

Once universities have <u>considered</u> your <u>application</u>, they'll make a <u>decision</u> about whether they're going to <u>offer</u> you a <u>place</u>. They can make you a <u>conditional offer</u>, an <u>unconditional offer</u> or <u>no offer</u>.

CONDITIONAL OFFER

- A <u>conditional offer</u> means you'll have to obtain <u>specific grades</u> or reach a <u>certain number</u> of <u>UCAS Tariff Points</u> to get on the course (see p.16).

- If you <u>meet</u> these conditions, you're <u>guaranteed a place</u> at the university.

- You'll <u>find out</u> whether you've got your place on <u>Results Day</u> (see p.73).

> You can withdraw an application for any course you no longer want to do, regardless of any offers you receive.

UNCONDITIONAL OFFER

- An <u>unconditional offer</u> means you are <u>guaranteed a place</u> on the course <u>if you accept</u> the offer — you won't have to achieve a specific set of grades or UCAS Tariff Points.

- You might still have to <u>sort other things</u> out, e.g. sending proof of your results.

- You should still <u>try your best</u> in your <u>exams</u> if you accept an unconditional offer — <u>they won't affect your place</u> on the course, but <u>future employers</u> may want to see how you did.

Unsuccessful Applications

1) If your application is <u>unsuccessful</u>, it means the university has decided <u>not to offer</u> you a place.

2) The university might give a <u>reason why</u> on UCAS Track. If they don't, you can <u>ask them</u> for a reason, but universities <u>don't have to give</u> you an <u>answer</u>.

3) If <u>none</u> of your applications were <u>successful</u>, you can try to find a course elsewhere using <u>UCAS Extra</u> (see page 75) or <u>Clearing</u> (see pages 76-77).

Offers

You'll Get Your Offers One by One

1) Universities make their <u>decisions</u> at <u>different times</u> — you <u>won't</u> find out about all of your offers <u>at the same time</u>.

2) When a university <u>makes a decision</u>, UCAS will <u>email you</u>. You can then log in to <u>UCAS Track</u> to see the <u>update</u>.

3) Universities have a few <u>deadlines</u> they have to meet when <u>responding</u> to your <u>application</u>:

   - If you <u>sent</u> your application by the <u>January deadline</u>, you should <u>hear back</u> by <u>early May</u>.
   - If you <u>sent</u> your application by the <u>June deadline</u>, you should <u>hear back</u> by <u>mid-July</u>.

4) If you <u>haven't had a response</u> by those dates, UCAS will <u>automatically mark</u> the application to that university as <u>unsuccessful</u>.

Lydia wished her friend's offer to go ice climbing had gotten lost in the post.

You Can Pick a Firm and an Insurance Choice

1) You don't need to make a decision as soon as you've had an offer — <u>you can wait</u> until you've <u>received responses</u> from <u>all the universities</u>.

2) Once you've heard back from <u>all of your choices</u>, you'll need to <u>pick</u> your <u>firm</u> and <u>insurance choices</u>:

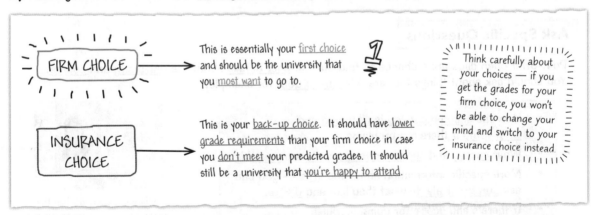

FIRM CHOICE → This is essentially your <u>first choice</u> and should be the university that you <u>most want</u> to go to.

INSURANCE CHOICE → This is your <u>back-up choice</u>. It should have <u>lower grade requirements</u> than your firm choice in case you <u>don't meet</u> your predicted grades. It should still be a university that <u>you're happy to attend</u>.

Think carefully about your choices — if you get the grades for your firm choice, you won't be able to change your mind and switch to your insurance choice instead.

3) If you <u>accept an unconditional offer</u> as your <u>firm choice</u>, you <u>won't be allowed to pick an insurance choice</u> — make sure <u>you're definitely happy</u> with an unconditional offer before you accept.

I'll always bring you fish.

I was expecting a conditional offer — but I was sent an unconditional otter...

Most offers will match the university course's entry requirements, but if you get an offer with conditions that you don't understand, ask the university to clarify so you know exactly what you're aiming for.

Post-Offer Open Days

Whether you have an offer that you're one hundred percent sure you want to accept, or you have one that you're not quite sure about, a post-offer open day is the event for you — I should really get a job in sales...

You Can Get A More In-Depth View of the University

1) Post-offer open days (also known as offer holder days or applicant visit days) are run by universities for applicants with an offer.

2) These events can be different from regular open days — each department might plan a schedule of activities to give you a more in-depth view of what studying there is like. They can include:

Course information sessions

These give you a detailed explanation of the modules and opportunities the course provides (e.g. placements or years abroad).

Sample lectures and seminars

These sessions give you a taste of what the teaching style and content is like.

Accommodation viewings

Some universities offer an overnight stay in their accommodation so you can get a feel for the area and what local student life is like.

Talks with tutors

You might be able to ask tutors and current students any questions that you have.

White Water Rafting

Okay, there might not be white water rafting, but there could be group activities with other applicants.

Remember any documents you're asked to bring (e.g. your booking confirmation).

Ask Specific Questions

Post-offer open days are a chance to find out the finer details about the university and course. You should ask about things that are relevant to you, for example:

- How the accommodation is allocated and what to do if there are problems.
- What access and support arrangements are available.
- More specific information about the area — you can ask current students what they like and dislike.
- If there's any scope for doing modules outside your chosen course.

Julia was bemused when the applicant asked where to get the best sourdough, stuffed crust, barbecue-base pizza on campus.

Time to take in the university atmosphere — smells like burnt pasta...

No matter how great a university sounds, the most important question you need an answer to is whether you can see yourself studying and living there for an extended period of time. Take time to make your decision.

Results Day

Results day can be stressful, and while you'll obviously hope that you get the grades you need, there's a chance things won't go to plan. If that happens, don't panic — there are options that you can explore.

Be Prepared **Before Results Day**

1) Have your <u>UCAS details</u> ready in case things don't quite go according to plan and you need to <u>get in touch</u> with **UCAS**.

2) Arrange <u>transport</u> to your school or college so you can <u>pick up</u> your exam <u>results</u> at the earliest opportunity. That way, you can <u>contact</u> universities as soon as possible if you need to.

You might be able to find out if you've got into university before collecting your results by checking UCAS Track.

3) <u>Plan ahead</u> for different <u>outcomes</u>:

If your grades <u>exceed your firm choice's offer</u>, you can go into <u>Adjustment</u> (see page 78).	If you get the grades for your <u>insurance choice</u> but not your firm choice, <u>UCAS</u> or your <u>insurance university</u> will <u>contact you</u>.	If you're <u>unsuccessful</u> with <u>both choices</u>, you can go into <u>Clearing</u> (see pages 76-77).

4) If you're <u>unavailable</u> on results day, you can give someone <u>nominated access</u> to your <u>UCAS account</u> so they can <u>speak on your behalf</u>. However, you should <u>try your best</u> to be available in case you need to find a new course.

Top Tips for Results Day

⭐ It's okay to <u>open your results on your own</u> if that makes you feel more comfortable.

⭐ <u>Be mindful</u> of others — it's okay to be pleased with your results, but <u>try not to flaunt your success</u> in case other people didn't do so well.

⭐ If your friends did well and you didn't, it might help to <u>stand away</u> from them so you can <u>focus on what you need to do next</u>.

⭐ Your <u>tutors and teachers</u> will be at results day and <u>they can help you decide what to do</u> if you didn't get the grades you wanted.

⭐ Try to <u>stay calm</u> if you have to <u>phone a university</u> — the <u>admissions team</u> will be doing their <u>best</u> to <u>help you</u>.

Billy spent time in his happy place to make sure he was relaxed on results day.

My pirate friend just got her exam results — she got high Cs...

If you don't manage to get into your firm or insurance choice and can't find a place you're happy with through Clearing, consider reapplying next year. There's no point going to a university that you aren't happy to attend.

After Results Day

After all your hard work, you've probably got a long list of fun things that you want to do before you start university. So, here's a page for you to make a list of all your big plans. I've even started it for you...

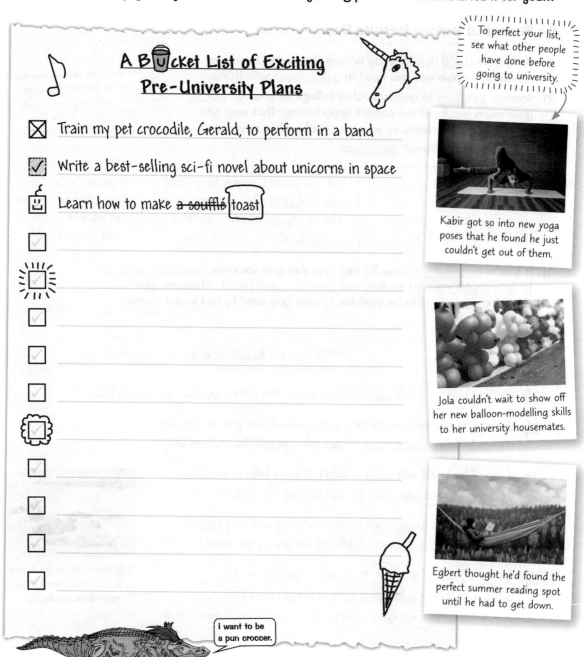

A Bucket List of Exciting
Pre-University Plans

☒ Train my pet crocodile, Gerald, to perform in a band

☑ Write a best-selling sci-fi novel about unicorns in space

☑ Learn how to make ~~a soufflé~~ toast

☐

☑

☐

☐

☐

☑

☐

☐

☐

☐

To perfect your list, see what other people have done before going to university.

Kabir got so into new yoga poses that he found he just couldn't get out of them.

Jola couldn't wait to show off her new balloon-modelling skills to her university housemates.

Egbert thought he'd found the perfect summer reading spot until he had to get down.

i want to be a pun croccer.

All of the most important things start with a list — just ask Father Christmas...

Personal experience has taught me that it's hard work trying to teach a crocodile to play guitar — but that's a story for another day. Your plans might be more conventional, but they're well deserved after all your work.

UCAS Extra

If you don't receive any offers from universities (or you decline all of the offers you get) and you've already used your five choices, you can submit an extra choice through UCAS Extra — think of it as an extra life.

UCAS Extra Lets You Apply For Another Course

1) UCAS Extra is a <u>free service</u> that's open between the <u>end of February</u> and the <u>beginning of July</u> — if you're eligible to use it, <u>UCAS</u> will <u>contact you</u> and grant you access to it in UCAS Track.

2) To <u>find a course</u> through UCAS Extra, use the <u>UCAS search tool</u> and filter for courses with <u>vacancies</u>. Make sure that you check the <u>entry requirements</u> for any course you might want to apply for.

3) You can only <u>apply</u> to <u>one course</u> at a time through UCAS Extra — to avoid wasting time, <u>contact the university directly</u> to make sure they'll <u>consider your application</u> before submitting it.

4) Once you apply to a course, the university has <u>21 days</u> to consider you. You then have options:

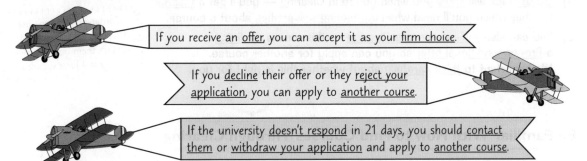

If you receive an <u>offer</u>, you can accept it as your <u>firm choice</u>.

If you <u>decline</u> their offer or they <u>reject your application</u>, you can apply to <u>another course</u>.

If the university <u>doesn't respond</u> in 21 days, you should <u>contact them</u> or <u>withdraw your application</u> and apply to <u>another course</u>.

5) There isn't a limit to the <u>number of times</u> you can go through this cycle during the UCAS Extra period.

6) Don't panic if you <u>don't find</u> a place before UCAS Extra <u>closes</u> — you can still apply to other courses through <u>Clearing</u> (there's more information on the next page).

> If you reject one of your original offers in the hope that you might find something better through UCAS Extra, you can't go back and accept that offer later.

UCAS Extra Uses Your Original Application

1) The <u>same application</u> that was sent to your original choices is used for courses found through UCAS Extra — this means you <u>won't</u> get to write a <u>new personal statement</u>.

2) If you want to <u>submit</u> a new personal statement, e.g. because you're applying for a completely different subject, you can <u>contact the university</u> you're applying to directly to see if they'll consider it.

As well as an extra UCAS choice, John also wanted extra popcorn.

Extra, extra, read all about it — oh, you already have...

Don't plan to use UCAS Extra when making your original course choices. View it like a spare pair of underwear — it's a useful backup plan that you hope you never have to use, but is there in case the unexpected happens...

Clearing

If you haven't found a place at university by the summer before you'd like to start, you can use Clearing. These pages will tell you what Clearing is and make sure that everything about it is... well, clear...

Clearing is a Final Chance to Find a University Place

1) Clearing is a UCAS service that helps to pair students who don't have any offers with universities that are looking to fill places.

2) You'll be eligible to use Clearing if you didn't get any offers, you didn't accept any offers, you didn't meet the entry requirements for your offers or you submitted your UCAS application after 30th June.

3) Clearing is open from early July, but you'll only be able to use it once you have your exam results.

4) UCAS Track will show you when you're in Clearing — you'll get a Clearing Number which you'll need when contacting universities about a course.

5) You can also self-release into Clearing — this means declining a firm unconditional offer so you can apply for another course. It's important to think carefully about whether this is right for you.

Sol suddenly realised he'd been looking for Clearing vacancies in the wrong place.

Conservatoires don't use Clearing — you'll need to contact them directly to see if they still have vacancies.

Be Familiar With How to Find Courses Through Clearing

- Make a shortlist of courses and research them in more depth.
- Talk to your tutors or careers advisors for help with this.

Use the UCAS search tool to find courses with vacancies.

ELEPHANT WHISPERING

- You'll need to give them your UCAS Personal ID and Clearing Number so they can look at your application.
- You should also ask any questions you have about the course and university.

Contact universities directly to see if they'll accept you.

Get informal offers from universities.

OFFER

- It can be useful to get a variety of offers before you choose to accept one.

Some universities run Clearing Open Days to help students decide if a course is right for them.

ACCEPT

Add your Clearing choice to UCAS Track.

- This counts as accepting an offer. You can only have one Clearing choice at a time, so make sure it's the one you want before you add it to UCAS Track.

Clearing

You Can Prepare For Clearing Before Results Day

It's a good idea to plan for Clearing even if you think you'll get the grades you need on results day.

1. ### Look at Courses in Advance

   Start looking for available courses in the days leading up to results day and make a list of course vacancies in order of interest. Note down the universities' phone numbers now so that you're ready to contact them if you end up entering Clearing.

2. ### Be Flexible and Realistic

   Consider alternative subjects and be sensible about any grade requirements you'll need. You could think about doing a foundation degree if you have a specific career in mind.

3. ### Be Ready to Contact Universities

   You'll have to talk to universities about your application and why you want to study there if you go through Clearing. Make a note of what you'll need as well as any questions you want to ask them beforehand, e.g. about modules and accommodation.

4. ### Consider Options Other than University

   Like with your original choices, you need to be sure that the course and university you find are right for you. There are other options that might be better than going to a university you're not sure about (see pages 4-7).

Clearing Can Be Stressful

You're not alone if you feel anxious about the thought of going through Clearing. Here are a few things to remember if you end up dealing with the process:

- Tens of thousands of students find their place through Clearing each year, which means that there's lots of support available.
- Empty places aren't a mark of poor quality — some of the highest-ranking universities might have vacancies if students they offered places to haven't met the entry requirements.
- It's okay to feel disappointed if you don't get your expected results — sometimes things don't go according to plan, but try to think of Clearing as another chance to reach your goals.
- Talk about how you're feeling — asking for help can make it easier to deal with any anxiety you feel about Clearing. You'll then be more prepared to make choices that you won't regret.

You could be Clearing the way for a new adventure...

Clearing obviously won't be your first choice, but it might turn out to be a blessing in disguise. You could end up doing something completely different to what you imagined, but this may open up new and exciting paths for you.

Adjustment

On results day, you might find you've done better than expected. If you have, you might be able to use UCAS Adjustment — a service that lets you switch to a university or course with higher entry requirements.

You Can Use Adjustment If You Do Better Than Expected

1. You'll be <u>eligible</u> for Adjustment if you <u>meet</u> and <u>exceed</u> the conditions of your offer, e.g. if your offer is ABB grades at A-Level and you achieve AAB. If you achieve AAC, this would not count as meeting and exceeding the conditions of your offer.

2. Adjustment is open from A-Level results day — you can <u>register using UCAS Track</u> once your conditional firm offer changes to an unconditional firm offer.

3. You <u>won't need to decline your firm offer</u> to register for Adjustment — you'll <u>keep your original choice</u> unless you find a new place.

4. Once you've registered, you have <u>five calendar days</u>, or until the end of the Adjustment period on <u>31st August</u>, to find a different place.

If you've changed your mind about what subject to study and you have the right grades, you can see if universities will accept you to study that subject instead.

Think Carefully When Using Adjustment

1) <u>Speak to your</u> tutors before you decide to use Adjustment — they might be able to help you decide whether it's the <u>right path for you</u>.

2) If you decide to use Adjustment, use the <u>UCAS search tool</u> to look for new courses. You'll need to <u>contact any universities directly</u> to find out if <u>there's space</u> on their course.

3) <u>Talk to a variety</u> of universities — make it clear that you're using Adjustment and give them your <u>UCAS Personal ID</u> so they can check you've met their <u>entry requirements</u>.

4) Have a <u>list of questions</u> ready to ask them and <u>be prepared to explain why</u> you want to change course at this stage.

5) When you're <u>certain</u> about a course, you'll need to <u>accept</u> a new offer <u>verbally</u>. Make sure you're <u>happy</u> with your choice — your original choice will be withdrawn once you agree to a different offer.

6) <u>After you've agreed</u> to a new offer, <u>UCAS Track will be updated</u> with your new firm choice. The university might also send more information.

Kitty spent a long time considering whether the adjustment process was right for her.

I used Adjustment to study drama instead — I wanted a change of scene...

Adjustment can be a great opportunity to find a different course. However, changing universities has an impact on your Student Finance and means you'll have to find new accommodation, so it's worth thinking about carefully.

Applying as an Ex-Student

If you've already left school or college, most of the university application process is the same, but there are a few more things that you might need to consider when applying. Here's a handy page of advice for you.

Contact Your Old School or College For Support

1) The <u>amount of support</u> available for former students <u>varies</u> across schools and colleges, but it's worth checking to see if you can get any <u>extra help with your application</u>, e.g. you might be able to get guidance for writing your personal statement.

2) If you're able to apply through your school or college, make sure you <u>get their buzzword</u> — this will let UCAS know that <u>your application is linked</u> to the centre.

Jamie wished he'd just asked his old school for their buzzword rather than trying to find it himself.

> If your school or college agrees to support your application, check if they have any internal deadlines you'll need to meet.

You'll Need to Find Someone to Write Your Reference

1) As an <u>individual student</u>, it's <u>your responsibility</u> to find someone who'll agree to write a reference to support your application. These are the people you could ask to do this:

A Former Tutor

If you've recently left school or college, contact your old tutor or teacher to check if they'd be happy to provide a reference for you, then enter their details and buzzword in the reference section of your UCAS application.

Someone from Work

If it's been a long time since you were in education, then your referee should be someone who knows you professionally. Once you've found a referee, you'll need to enter their email address and phone number into your UCAS application.

> Don't ask a family member, friend, partner or ex-partner — your application could be cancelled if your reference is written by someone who only knows you personally.

2) If your <u>referee</u> is someone from work, they'll <u>receive an email</u> with a link and password to the UCAS website, as well as instructions. Once they've confirmed their identity, they can write your reference.

3) <u>Give your referee plenty of time</u> to write your reference and <u>keep in touch</u> with them so you know when it's complete. When they've finished it, you can <u>pay for your application</u> and <u>submit it</u>.

A benefit of being an ex-student is that you often already have your results...

Don't worry if your old school or college doesn't offer you much support — you can still write a fantastic UCAS application with the help of other resources, such as this marvellous book that's right before your very eyes.

Index

Index

Top 10 Ultimate Application Tips

Repeat these tips like they're the lyrics to that catchy new pop song and you'll be on your way to greatness.

  CGP University

- Start planning for university as soon as possible.

- Work out how you'll fund your studies.

- Research universities and courses thoroughly.

- Find ways to stand out from the crowd early.

- Make an application timetable.

- Get advice and feedback on your application.

- Write numerous drafts of your personal statement.

- Finish your application with plenty of time to spare.

- Choose a university that you're happy with.

- Stay calm! A great application takes time, but if you plan carefully you'll be at university before you know it!

Certified Degree in Getting to University
ish